THE SOVEREIGNTY OF GOD

THE SOVEREIGNTY OF GOD

The Proceedings
of
The First American Calvinistic Conference

Edited by

JACOB T. HOOGSTRA, TH.D. President

Paterson Y.M.C.A.
and
Sixth Reformed Church of Paterson, NJ

June 27 – 30, 1939

SOLID GROUND CHRISTIAN BOOKS
BIRMINGHAM, ALABAMA USA

Solid Ground Christian Books
PO Box 660132
Vestavia Hills AL 35266
205-443-0311
sgcb@charter.net
www.solid-ground-books.com

THE SOVEREIGNTY OF GOD
The Proceedings of the First American Calvinistic Conference

Edited by Jacob T. Hoogstra

Taken from the 1939 edition by Zondervan Publishing House
of Grand Rapids, Michigan

Cover image is Mt. McLoughlin, Oregon by Ric Ergenbright.
See all Ric's work at www.ricergenbright.com

Cover design by Borgo Design
Contact them at borgogirl@bellsouth.net

ISBN- 978-159925-191-2

PREFACE

The Eastern Ministers' Conference appointed the Rev. J. J. Hiemenga, the Rev. Jacob Van Bruggen, its secretary, and the Rev. Dr. Jacob T. Hoogstra to investigate whether or not there is sufficient enthusiasm to realize an American Calvinistic Conference. Upon hearing a favorable report, this conference authorized its committee to carry out the plan suggested. The Rev. M. E. Broekstra, and later on, the Rev. Lawrence Borst were added to the committee. At a later meeting, the Eastern Ministers' Conference included the Rev. Dr. Clarence Bouma, professor in Calvin Seminary, as honorary vice-president. This distinction would have been given also to the Rev. Dr. S. C. Nettinga, professor in Western Seminary, for his advice and interest, had not his life been cut short. The Rev. J. J. Hiemenga functioned as president of this committee, the Rev. Jacob Van Bruggen as secretary, and the Rev. Dr. Jacob T. Hoogstra as corresponding secretary.

This program committee was authorized to appoint Mr. Gerrit Egedy, Mr. John Teitsma, and Mr. George Breur, attorney-at-law, to constitute the Social-Music Committee. This committee executed its task admirably. With the splendid coöperation of all who were asked to participate, our conferees received the desired hospitality and our public meetings were inspirational centers of song and worship.

Mr. John Zuidema, of the Prospect Park National Bank, Paterson, New Jersey, gladly transacted the finances of our conference.

Preface

It was a great satisfaction to all that at the final meeting of the Conference Program Committee it was decided upon motion to express as our judgment that the conference was a success. In this we do not seek human praise. Ours was the joy to labor in the presence of the sovereign God, Who reads the hearts and sees the doings of men. We sincerely hope that our conference may be instrumental in making man bow before his Maker. May this volume, *The Proceedings of the American Calvinistic Conference*, enlarge the conference's scope of influence.

JACOB T. HOOGSTRA

LIST OF MEMBERS OF THE CONFERENCE HELD IN THE PATERSON Y.M.C.A.*

Aalders, (Rev.) Gerhard Charles. Th.D., Nassaulaan 33, Hilversum, Netherlands; professor in the Free University, Amsterdam, Netherlands; author. Conference speech: "The Sovereignty of God and the Word of God"

Allis, (Rev.) Oswald T., B.D., M.A., Ph.D., D.D., University of Pennsylvania, Princeton Seminary and University, Berlin University; care of Miss M. E. Allis, The Genoa, Philadelphia, Pa.; teacher and writer

Beversluis, Henry, A.B., Calvin College, 365 N. 8th St., Paterson, N. J.; student

Blackburn, (Rev.) John C., 2416 Devine St., Columbia, S. C.; minister, author

Borst, (Rev.) Lawrence James, A.B., Th.B., Hope College and Western Theological Seminary, 141 Hamilton Ave., Passaic, N. J.; minister; member of Program Committee

Bos, John R., A.B., A.M., Calvin College, University of Michigan, 99 North 16th St., Prospect Park. N. J.; principal

Botbyl, (Rev.) M. B., Christian Reformed College and Seminary, Monsey, N. Y.; minister

Bouma, Annette. A.B., Calvin College, Montclair State Teachers College, 52 Summer St., Passaic, N. J.; teacher

Bouma, (Rev.) Hessel, B.D., Calvin, McCormick, Princeton, 52 Summer St., Passaic, N. J.; minister

Breen, (Rev.) Oliver. A.B., Th.B., Calvin College and Seminary, 44 Wickham Ave., Goshen, N. Y.; minister

Breur, George A., LL.B., New Jersey Law School, Alps Road, Preakness, N. J.; lawyer; secretary of Social-Music Committee

*Only those who have attended the Paterson Y.M.C.A. meetings have been listed. Some failed to register.

Broekstra, (Rev.) M. E., Kampen Theological School, Netherlands; Western Theological Seminary, 172 Haledon Ave., Paterson, N. J.; minister; member of Program Committee

Burggraaff, (Rev.) Winfield, A.B., Th.B., Th.D., Hope, Western Theological Seminary, Free University, Amsterdam, Huguenot Park, Staten Island, N. Y.; minister and writer

Cole, Agnes, 168 Harrison St., Passaic, N. J.; teacher

DeBeer, (Rev.) Dirk, Calvin College and Seminary, 247 Lafayette Ave., Passaic, N. J.; minister

DeMoor, (Rev.) Leonard, A.B., A.M., S.T.M., Ph.D., Hope College, University of Michigan, Western Theological Seminary, Harvard University, Hartford Seminary, Marburg University, Germany; Hudsonville, Mich.; minister, professor, and writer. Conference address: "The Sovereignty of God and Philosophy"

DeJonge, (Rev.) A. W., Western Theological Seminary, 159 N. First St., Paterson, N. J.; minister

Egedy, Gerrit, 160 Buena Vista Ave., Hawthorne, N.J., Gideon; salesman; president of Social-Music Committee

Frieling, (Rev.) Harke, Calvin College, Western Theological Seminary, 6 Auburn St., Paterson, N. J.; minister

Gray, (Rev.) Richard W., A.B., Th.B., Wheaton College, Westminster Seminary, 7 Franklin Ave., Montclair, N. J.; minister

Greenfield, (Rev.) Charles, A.B., Th.B., Calvin Seminary, Terra Ceia, N. C.; minister

Greenway, (Rev.) Leonard, Th.D., 841 Burton St., S. W., Grand Rapids, Mich.; minister. Conference address: "The Sovereignty of God and Human Responsibility"

Heneveld, (Rev.) George G., A.B., A.M., Hope and Western Theological Seminary, Wyckoff, N. J.; minister

Heyns, Garrett, Ph.D., Calvin College, University of Michigan, Box 500, Ionia, Mich.; one time principal of Christian Schools; State warden. Conference address: "The Sovereignty of God and Political Life"

Hiemenga, (Rev.) J. J., A.M., B.D., Calvin, Columbia University, Rochester Seminary, 55 Haledon Ave., Paterson, N. J.; president of Calvin College (1919-25); minister; President of Program Committee

Hommes, Richard, Calvin College, 137 E. 19th St., Paterson, N. J.; principal

Hoogstra, (Rev.) Jacob T., A.B., Th.M., Th.D., Calvin College, Calvin Seminary, Princeton Seminary, University of Tubingen, Union Seminary, New York, Biblical Seminary in New York; minister; president of the Conference

Keyser, Peter, 38 Arlington Ave., Hawthorne, N. J.; salesman, Gideon

Kirsch, (Rev.) Charles E., A.B., Th.D., Th.M., Lafayette College, Princeton Theological Seminary, University of Edinburgh, 2722 Fenwick Ave., Baltimore, Md.; minister

Klerekoper, (Rev.) Joseph, Amsterdam University, 167 Hadley Ave., Clifton, N. J.; minister

Kooistra, (Rev.) Elbert, Calvin College, Calvin Seminary, Midland Park, N. J.; minister

Kromminga, (Rev.) D. H., Grand Rapids, Mich.; preacher and professor of Church History. Conference address: "The Sovereignty of God and Barthianism"

Kruithof, (Rev.) Bastian, A.M., Calvin College and Seminary, University of Michigan, Columbia; 91 Third Ave., Hawthorne, N. J.; minister and author

Macleod, (Rev.) John, M.A., (Abdn.) 1891, D.D. (Abdn.) 1927, 3 Rillbank Terrace, Edinburgh, Scotland; professor of Theology and College Principal, Free Church of Scotland. Conference addresses: "The Sovereignty of God—A Dogmatic Study"; "God's Sovereign Choice of the Younger Son"

Matheson, (Rev.) William, University College, Toronto; Chesley, Ontario; minister. Conference address: "The Sovereignty of God and Christian Ethics"

Meeter, H. Henry, Th.D., Calvin, Princeton Seminary, Free University of Amsterdam, Holland; 1045 Fuller Ave., S.E., Grand Rapids, Mich.; teacher and author

Meeter, John E., A.B., Th.B., Th.M., Th.Drs., Calvin College and Seminary, Princeton Seminary, Free University at Amsterdam, Harvard Divinity School, 239 Park Ave., Chambersburg, Pa.; assistant professor of Bible

Meeter, Mrs. John, A.B., Calvin College, University of Michigan, 239 Park Ave., Chambersburg, Pa.

Mierop, Nella, D.L., Passaic High, N. J., State College for Women. 54 Irving Place, Passaic, N. J.; Christian school teacher

Mosser, (Rev.) Cameron, D.L., A.B., S.T.B., Taylor University, Upland, Ind., The Biblical Seminary in New York, 257 Liberty St., Newburgh, N. Y.; minister

Mosser, Mrs. C., D.L., Biblical Seminary in New York, 257 Liberty St., Newburgh, N. Y.

Murray, (Prof.) John, M.A., Th.M., Glasgow University, Princeton Theological Seminary, Edinburgh University, Westminster Seminary, Philadelphia, Pa. Professor, co-editor of Westminster Journal. Conference address: "The Sovereignty of God, a Biblical Theological Study"

Reynolds, Stephen M., A.B., Th.B., Ph.D., Miami University, Princeton Theological Seminary, 33 Jefferson Road, Princeton, N. J.; assistant professor of Old Testament

Reynolds, (Rev.) Walter H., A.M., D.D., College of Wooster, McCormick Seminary, 33 Jefferson Road, Princeton, N. J.; retired minister

Robinson, (Prof.) William Childs, A.B., A.M., B.D., Th.M., Th.D., D.D., Roanoke College, University of South Carolina, Columbia and Princeton Theological Seminaries, Harvard University, University of Basel, Decatur, Ga.; professor Historical Theology. Conference address: "The Sovereignty of God and American Attitudes"

Rooks, Albert J., Hope, University of Michigan, Bonn University, Germany, 737 Benjamin Ave., Grand Rapids, Mich.; dean Calvin College

Rosengrant, (Rev.) Harry W., A.B., B.D., Th.D., Syracuse University, Drew Theological Seminary, 379 Fifteenth Ave., Paterson, N. J.; minister

Selles, Peter A., 50 Graves Place, Holland, Mich.

Stam, Peter, 34 Broadway, Paterson, N. J.; missionary

Tanis, James, 101 Haledon Ave., Paterson N. J.

Timmer, Johanna, A.B., A.M., Calvin College, Calvin Seminary, University of Chicago, University of Michigan, Presbyterian Seminary in Chicago, 619 Prince St., Grand Rapids, Mich.; until September, 1939, dean of women of Calvin College; field worker and future teacher of The Reformed Bible Institute

Van Bruggen, (Rev.) Jacob, Calvin College, Calvin Seminary, Westminster Seminary; secretary of the Program Committee and Conference; now missionary to the Navajo Indians, Crown Point, N. M.

Van de Kieft, (Rev.) J. M., A.B., B.D., Calvin College and Seminary, Princeton Seminary, 193 N. 9th St., Paterson, N. J.; minister

Van Dyke, (Rev.) P., Calvin College and Seminary, Central College, Pella, Iowa; Columbia University; 262 N. 7th St., Paterson, N. J.; minister and author

Van Halsema, (Rev.) E., A.B., Th.D. S.T.M., Calvin, Union Seminary, New York, 219 Myrtle Ave., Passaic, N. J.; minister and correspondent

Van Houte, (Rev.) Daniel, Calvin and Westminster, Pownal, Maine; minister

Van Hoff, Gertrude, A.B., Calvin College, Goffle Hill Road, Midland Park, N. J.; student

Van Pernis, (Rev.) Gerard M., Academy in the Netherlands, Hope, 310 Burgess Place, Clifton, N. J.; minister and editor

Vincze, (Rev.) Charles, B.D., Th.M., S.T.D., Sarospatak, Debrecen (Hungary), Princeton, 331 Kirkland Place, Perth Amboy, N. J.; minister and editor. Conference address: "The Future of Calvinism in America"

Walkotten, (Rev.) John, Calvin College; 13 North Straight St., Paterson, N. J.; minister

Westervelt, (Rev.) John A., 18 Tonawanda Road, Glen Rock, N. J.; emeritus pastor

Woolley, Paul, A.B., Th.B., Th.M., Princeton University, Princeton Theological Seminary, Westminster College, Cambridge; University of Berlin; 152 W. Horlter St., Philadelphia, Pa.; teacher of theology and co-editor of Westminster Theological Journal

Wyngaarden, Martin J., A.B., B.D., A.M., Ph.D., Calvin College; Occidental College; University of Washington, Seattle; Calvin Seminary; Princeton Seminary, Princeton University, University of Pennsylvania, Philadelphia; Yale University; 1144 Chippewa Drive, Grand Rapids, Mich.; professor of Old Testament Interpretation and author; ordained minister

Table of Contents

WELCOME ADDRESS

The Rev. J. J. Hiemenga, A.M., B.D.

It is not at all strange that in our days the human mind has to reconsider the theories and conclusions of the past. The world has undergone tremendous changes and finds itself in a constant uncertainty. At present we are speaking in connection with the World's Fair here in New York about the "achievements" of the last decade, but the solution of the world's problems, politically, socially, and religiously, has not yet been found. The world is still groping about in the dark. Nor is it at all surprising that in this present stage of uncertainty, the market is flooded with new theories presented as remedies for prevailing diseases. And here is the challenge of the church of God, for it is unto her that the only remedy has been committed.

It is without doubt due to the challenge that there has come about a revival of interest in Calvinism. It has made its appearance beyond the Atlantic Ocean in several European countries as well as in South Africa and here in America. We Calvinists have faith in the dynamic power of a consistent, uncompromising appeal to "the law and the testimony," to the infallibility of the Word of God and its application to every sphere of life. Our purpose is to meet the challenge of the day

11

and to study and to reemphasize and to propagate our Calvinistic principles.

Our first Calvinistic Conference in America has a brief history. The honor of suggesting such a conference belongs to Dr. J. Hoogstra, of Englewood, N. J. It was at his suggestion that a committee was appointed by the Ministers Conference of the Reformed and Christian Reformed churches in the East. Much of the preparatory work has also been done by Dr. Hoogstra. And while it has been my privilege to serve as president of the Committee up until now, I feel that Dr. Hoogstra, because of his interest in this cause and his untiring efforts, is entitled to the honor of being president of the first American Calvinistic Conference. I present this as a motion for your approval.

John J. Hiemenga

ACCEPTANCE OF THE PRESIDENCY

The Rev. Dr. J. T. Hoogstra

To the members of the First American Calvinistic Conference:*

In spite of the fact that Americans may be working overtime to bring about church unions, we do not feel any necessity for apologizing for the First American Calvinistic Conference. Reasons for this attitude will be stated presently. We do feel, however, that the acceptance of the presidency of this conference requires a little explanation. The program committee has overruled my tendency to shirk from this type of responsibility. I have allowed myself to be persuaded to accept, knowing that the committee desired to show its appreciation for the work I was privileged to do. Even now I feel that others more distinctive in Calvinistic accomplishments should enjoy this honor. I wish to thank the Committee most sincerely for this appreciation.

Although all members have put their soul into this work, I am sure no one will think ill of me if I remind this conference that we owe a special debt to the president of the program committee for his encouragements in critical moments, and for his help at all hours of

*Colossians 2 must be read with this address.

the day, the Rev. J. J. Hiemenga. May I say at this
very opening meeting that I appreciate the confidence
the Eastern Ministers Conference has placed in us. This
conference shares with the committee the vision of ad-
vancing Calvinism in this, our age. Not every ministers'
conference would have dared to encourage this project
of faith.

Before this conference is over, I shall have more to
say about the committees and the individuals who have
given of their time and their money to make this enter-
prize a success. All that I can say at this time is that I
sincerely pray that the Lord of the harvest will graciously remember every participant. This prayer includes all who have come to spend a few days together.
We assure you that our Eastern constituency welcomes
you as fellow-heirs of the faith. We hope you will
return to your homes to go forward in the faith of
our Lord to greater deeds of consecration in the age
when souls are homesick for eternity but find no rest
in the panaceas they have produced.

The source from which our acceptance speech is
taken is the second chapter of the Epistle to the Colossians. To know the sovereign God is to live consciously
in the presence of the God of the Scriptures. This
chapter tells us at least three things. Each day our
faces must be toward the throne above. Only Christians
can look heavenward, for they have the Christ, "in
whom dwelleth the fulness of the Godhead bodily."
He that hath seen the Christ hath seen the Father. Only
Christ can draw us to the Father. Besides, we are members of the covenant that God made with Abraham.
Therein lies our obligation. We also have a challenge
in this chapter. Our exalted Christ has made an open
display of defeated anti-Christian thoughts and deeds,

whether in man or in demons. He is the triumphant Christ, in Whom the fulness of the Godhead dwelleth. These, then, are the three reasons that make apologies for a Calvinistic conference at this time inane and superfluous. The Christ Whom we love is the fulness of the Godhead; the covenant is the obligation that is ours; and the victory of our Lord is our hope and inspiration to go forward in His name.

Paul commends the preaching of Epaphras. His simple exhortations accepted most likely by the majority of the congregation pointed sinners to the all-sufficient Christ. Certain philosophers in the congregation insinuated that Epaphras lacked intellectual profoundness. His was the simple message of faith. Theirs was the depth of knowledge and of wisdom that knew the manifestation of the Godhead in angels and other creatures. They had in addition to Christ angels and creatures. Epaphras had only the Christ by faith. Although Paul does not in any way give a blanket condemnation of all pagan philosophy in this chapter, he does criticize this specific school in a way that teaches us what Paul thought of similar attempts. Epaphras or the philosopher! Christ only or Christ plus someone or something! Yes, the story of the Middle Ages is already whispered here in this city of Colosse. Faith or reason! Our thinking according to man or according to the Christ! Can the philosopher "in Adam" help the preacher who wishes to be only "in Christ"?

Paul is not aware of the struggle that is ahead of him. We know St. Augustine, the Christian thinker, and Augustine, the Neo-Platonist. Anselm and Abelard thought all the truths of faith could be established and arrived at by some pure reason. Even in Islamic thinking, especially in a man such as Averroes, we see the contest between theology and philosophy. Soon the universities were teaching that there were two standards of truth—the theological and the philosophical. This is a story that brings to the foreground names more or less familiar, such as Occam, Thomas Aquinas, Luther, Calvin, Pomponatius, the Deists, Kant, Hegel, Schleiermacher, Ritschl, Hermann, Karl Barth, Emil Brunner, as well as our Calvinistic philosophers, Dooyeweerd and Vollenhoven. Paul has only one answer—all truth is truth, for Christ is "the fulness of the Godhead bodily." There is no truth that is of absolute value unless it is related to the risen Christ. He is the source of all our knowledge. Unless our particular branch of learning and endeavor, whether philosophy or theology, ethics or psychology, is related to Him, we have missed the mark. Everything must be seen in the light of and related to the triumphant Lord. Paul, with one sentence, denounces any attempt to build upon human reason as an ultimate source of thought or authority. There is no such thing as a neutral reason. Reason is either "in Adam" or "in Christ." This, I take it, is the Calvinistic philosophy of education. So Calvin, Kuyper, and our contemporary Calvinistic philosophers. We never approach a system unless Christ is the very center of that system. This, then, is our God-given task today. We must relate our entire life to the Christ. Insofar as we do not, we are sinning, and our life is a failure. Christ is our answer; the working out of that answer in our life is our task.

If this were a dissertation in exegesis, we might have to establish the meaning of the word "bodily." What does Paul mean when he says that the fulness of the Godhead dwells in Christ "bodily"? Even the latest commentators do not agree. J. A. C. Van Leeuwen thinks of "bodily" in contrast with the shadows of the Old Testament. If so, the Godhead dwells in Christ in reality, not in shadows. The tabernacle was the dwelling-place in shadows. A. S. Peake construes this concept as "organically." That is, the philosophers divided the manifestation of the Godhead among the angels and the spirits they worshiped. Paul, then, replies that all truth is organically in the Christ, and that the Godhead cannot be proportioned among the angelic hosts. Whatever exegetical differences there may be among competent expositors, the fact remains that Christ is the all-sufficient, undivided fountain of all education, religion, worship, and activity. If we are to bow before the sovereign God, we must do so in the Christ.

This truth is as applicable today as in the time of St. Paul. I can only suggest, for tonight Dr. W. C. Robinson will discourse on the "Sovereignty of God and American Attitudes." It is my conviction that many American attitudes attempt to entertain other sources besides the Christ of the Scriptures. May I illustrate? Is the church a given institution of God or is it man's attempt to organize the religious forces to save mankind? For us, the answer is simple. We who have the *living* Christ are called to obey Him and through obedience in His name are summoned to worship the sovereign God. This question regarding the nature of the church is the great obstacle in church union. Well may it be so, for fundamentally the question is whether the church is the church of grace or of human endeavors. Is the *living* Christ calling His own or should we add foreign fires to the altars of God? Another illustration perhaps may drive the same point home. The philosophers of Paul's day taught that the Godhead was divided among the Christ and the angels. Christ plus something else! Although not in the crude fashion of long ago, we have the same situation when we aver that the dogmas of atonement and salvation are of European importation but that we must add our American philosophy to give the kingdom of God the forgotten aspect of expansion.

Again we are faced with the same question: How can we add to the all-sufficient Christ something that is in very nature anti-Christian? Christ is the fountain of truth. We Americans have developed the doctrine that we make truth as we proceed. What satisfies mankind is truth for us. If we try to add to the doctrines of Scripture that truth is made and that our modern gospel is added to the gospel of Christ, then we are virtually saying that Christ is the truth but that He is in need of the additional truth we discover. Either Christ is all-sufficient or He is not the perfect Christ.

We must not silence these philosophical differences of the day. It is an easy matter to say that this is just philosophy and that the average man does not care about it, but the fact remains we cannot accept Cain and Abel in the same church. Jacob is still fighting Esau. Church efficiency to fight Communism is only a sham the moment these differences are ignored. If we err in the fundamentals, we forsake the Christ. Let us insist upon a philosophy that begins with the exalted Christ and that dedicates all things to His honor. Every thought must be held in subjection to Him. Christ shares this glory with no one. This opportunity to come together as a conference—for the church cannot assume this academic and social task—is a God-given privilege to help one another to return home with renewed enthusiasm. What He says we will do. He comes first.

We shall not cater to the changing codes of morality. His word shall remain forever and ever.

Besides being a privilege, we may speak of this work in a stronger fashion. It is an obligation. The doctrine of the covenant is peculiar to the Reformed faith. Why it should have developed in the Reformed bosom is not hard to see. The Reformed faith has always emphasized the doctrine of the sovereignty of God. There can be no doubt but that it required the Reformed genius to doscover and to relate the doctrine of the sovereignty of God to the doctrine of the covenant. God makes a covenant with us. As a sovereign He alone prescribes the conditions upon which man may commune with Him. We cannot disobey this covenant without realizing that we have sinned against our Sovereign. He speaks; we must believe and obey.

We ought not to forget this covenant today. Covenant means obligation. It also spells grace and love. We think of the sovereign Love that promises us and even our newly born infants that we have the name of the triune God engraven on our foreheads as a sign and seal that we are members of His church.

Undoubtedly the philosophers in the chapter under consideration thought that they had prerogatives since they were of Jewish extraction. Should not the Gentile church lend an ear to those who were of the Old Testament? Should not prestige count for something? Paul says this is not the case. The truth is that circumcision with hands is obsolete. Today it has no advantages. But the "Christ-circumcision" is ever new. That is, we have a circumcision made without hands. **Our circumcision places us in the same covenant, only we enjoy a higher and a richer share in that covenant. Our circumcision that we have is our baptism. Our baptism has** taken the place of the Old Testament circumcision. We are obliged before God to live this covenant life. We are obliged to serve the Christ in all His fulness. We must serve Him everywhere. This is our human responsibility. If the doctrine of the sovereignty of God is not merely a traditional slogan, let us live our covenant obligation. He has spoken graciously, to be sure, but still as our sovereign Lord. Our pulpits should proclaim this truth; our classrooms should create this covenant atmosphere; and our lives and souls should be covenant conscious. We are circumcized without hands in the very baptism and resurrection of the Christ.

Having this amazing source of knowledge and duty, having this obligation as covenant children, to serve God by relating all things to Him, we feel there is a challenge for us today. Faith says this should be self-evident. If we truly believe all that we know the Bible says of the victory of the Christ, we shall not hesitate to go into the world to live our convictions. Christ has made an open display of His defeated enemies. His enemies of today will suffer the same disgrace their comrades did in the men Paul denounces. We must as a group of Bible-believing Christians, especially of the Reformed faith, sound the apologetic note. We begin with the Christ. We apply the Christ. We show the world our true beginning—God, through the Christ. We must show to the world that it must, through its aimless logic, always idolize man and that it must of necessity be without a goal or a hope. Whether the world will hear or forbear, we must show that the Christ is the only satisfaction for time and eternity. He has defeated the philosophies of chance and compromise. He has given us His Spirit. It is our sincerest prayer that these days may not be spent in vain. We do not look upon them as feasting upon great truths for the sake of abstract learning. We wish to know to serve. We acquire to do.

May I conclude with this thought? Unfortunately we have to call ourselves Calvinists. Our prayer is for the entire Zion of God. Even today we are convening as Calvinists for the sake of the entire church of God. The point is that the Reformed faith and the Calvinistic philosophy are the truest and most comprehensive expression of Christianity we know of. This conviction marks us off from others who differ with us; so we must indicate this difference by some name history has given to us. We think that John Calvin and his spiritual descendants have been blessings of God in opening for us the Scriptures. We may dislike the necessity of calling ourselves by a human name, but we cannot escape it. We grant that others have the same right to think that their system of thought is the very best. If they did not, they would not have the moral right to exist as Lutherans or as Methodists, as the case may be. There is no reason, however, that we cannot in Christian love study what other branches of the kingdom of our Lord are discovering in the Bible as the Word of God. Let the Methodists and the Lutherans get together to study the Bible. Let us all compare notes. We feel that we serve the entire Christian family, if we study our own position. Let us seek to persuade the church of God that our truths are Biblical. We must tell the world and other Christians what we believe and why we believe the way we do. This, I take it, was also the position of the late Dr. Herman Bavinck. To benefit the church, we must teach and live the great doctrines we hold essential. Perhaps we can help the church at large in thinking and formulating the doctrines of the return of Christ. We can defend our convictions concerning the Bible. We may even clarify the atmosphere by explaining our stand regarding the social implications of the Christian message without resorting to a social gospel. We can make our own contributions, distinctive, to be sure, but our prayer is the blessing upon the entire catholic church. We are not met here as schismatics. We are soldiers of the truth, obligated to serve the risen Lord, challenged to fight Satan in the name of our Sovereign Lord, blessed with the hope that all the children of our Father will listen to what we say and teach in order that we may unite against the world, not in efficiency nor in compromise, but in conviction and in truth. This has always been considered the genuine ecumenicity.

Should we, in 1939, entertain fears that our faith is possibly wrong? Across the mountains, miles of telephone poles carry wires from central station to the farthest hamlet. Across the ages, from the publican before the Temple and the harlot at Jesus' feet, the giant St. Paul, Augustine, Luther, Calvin, Kuyper, Bavinck, and all the saints of God in the sacred moment of prayer, stand like huge telephone poles across the mountains of history, bearing this one wire that unites them all—"saved by grace." I thank Thee, Lord, for every iota of salvation. I love Thee because Thou hast first loved me. God chose me: I did not choose Him. And this *is* Calvinism.

FOUNDATIONAL STUDIES

A BIBLICAL THEOLOGICAL STUDY

THE REV. PROF. JOHN MURRAY

THE sovereignty of God I take to be the absolute authority, rule, and government of God in the whole of that reality that exists distinct from Himself in the realms of nature and of grace. It is a concept that respects His relation to other beings and to all other being and existence. It is, therefore, a relative concept, or a concept of relation.

If God possesses and exercises this absolute authority, rule, and government, the necessary presupposition of it is the *oneness*, or *unity*, of God. It is a fact to which Scripture bears constant witness in a great variety of contexts because it is a truth that underlies and determines the whole superstructure of divine revelation.

An examination of this witness will show that it is not mere uniqueness or supremacy or even transcendence in the realm of Deity. It is not as if there were a host of lesser deities over whom God is supreme and therefore demands from us supreme worship and devotion. It is rather that He alone is God. "The Lord he is God; there is none else besides him." "He is God in heaven above, and upon the earth beneath: there is none else" (Deut. 4: 35, 39). "Hear, O Israel: the Lord our God is one Lord" (Deut. 6:4). "See now that I,

25

even I, am he, and there is no god with me" (Deut. 32:39). "Thou art the God, even thou alone, of all the kingdoms of the earth" (II Kings 19:15).

It is significant that it is precisely this line of Old Testament witness that is appealed to by our Lord as the answer to the question, "What commandment is the first of all?" "The first . . . is, Hear, O Israel; the Lord our God is one Lord" (Mark 12:29). And the necessary consequence for us is, "Thou shalt love the Lord thy God with all thy heart, and with all thy soul, and with all thy mind, and with all thy strength" (Mark 12:30). "Thou shalt worship the Lord thy God, and him only shalt thou serve" (Matt. 4:10). The pivotal character of the oneness of God appears, for example, in Paul's Epistle to the Romans, when it is made the hinge upon which turns and hangs no less important a doctrine than that of justification by faith. "Or is he the God of the Jews only? Is he not also of the Gentiles? Yes, of the Gentiles also: seeing it is one God, which shall justify the circumcision by faith, and uncircumcision through faith" (Rom. 3: 29-31). And again in the First Epistle to the Corinthians, the foundation that "to us there is but one God, the Father, of whom are all things, and we in him; and one Lord Jesus Christ, by whom are all things, and we by him" (I Cor. 8:6) is the first principle regulative of worship.

The concept of divine sovereignty presupposes also the fact of *creation*, that is, the origination of all other existence by the fiat of God. The moment we posit the existence of anything independent of God in its derivation of factual being, in that moment we have denied the divine sovereignty. For even should we grant that now or at some point God has assumed or gained absolute control over it, the moment we allow the existence of anything outside of His fiat as its principle or origination and outside of His government as the principle of its continued existence, then we have eviscerated the *absoluteness* of the divine authority and rule.

Scripture is paramountly conscious of this fact, and so its witness to the absolutely originative activity of God is pervasive. It does not depend wholly upon a few well-known texts, however important these may be.

Perhaps no word expresses it more pointedly than that of the Psalm: "By the word of the Lord were the heavens made; and all the host of them by the breath of his mouth" (Ps. 33:6). The import is that the word, or breath of God, breath being the symbol of His almighty, creative will, is the antecedent, or prior cause, of all that is. "For he spake, and it was done; he commanded, and it stood fast" (vs. 9). This mode of statement harks back to the first chapter of Genesis, where on some eight occasions the successive steps of the creative drama are introduced with the formula, "and God said."

God made heaven and earth; by His Spirit the heavens were garnished; He laid the foundations of the earth; by wisdom He founded the earth; by understanding He established the heavens; His hands stretched out the heavens, and all their host He commanded; heaven and earth, His hand made, and so all those things came to be; He made the sea and the dry land; He is the first and the last, the Alpha and Omega; He is the beginning of creation; by His will, heaven and earth were, and were created (II Kings 19:15; Job 26:13; 38:4; Prov. 3:19; Isa. 42:5; 44:6; 45:12; 66:2; Jonah 1:9; Rev. 1:8; 3:14; 4:8).

The piety on which the Scripture places its imprimatur as true piety, we find, rests upon, and is necessarily suffused with, the recognition of God's creatorhood. The address to God in adoration, prayer, and praise begins with it; the address to men in law and gospel rests upon it. The faith that is "the substance of things hoped for, the evidence of things not seen," the faith through which the catalogue of saints had witness borne to them that they were righteous is the faith through which "we understand that the worlds were framed by the word of God, so that things which are seen were not made of things which do appear" (Heb. 11:3). And when Paul made his appeal to the idolatrous Athenians that God now commandeth men that they should all, everywhere repent, he began his address by saying, "God that made the world and all things therein, seeing that he is Lord of heaven and earth, dwelleth not in temples made with hands" (Acts 17:24).

If the sovereignty of God rests upon the fact of His oneness and upon the fact of creation, it may be said to consist, first of all, in the right of dominion and rule over all and in the fact of universal possession. The Psalm sounds this note succinctly. "The earth is the Lord's, and the fulness thereof" (Ps. 24:1). The prophets do the same when they affirm that He is "the God of the whole earth" and as the "Most High ruleth in the kingdom of men, and giveth it to whomsoever he will" (Isa. 54:5; Dan. 4: 17, 25). In the formula of Melchizedek and of Abraham, He is the "possessor of heaven and earth" (Gen. 14: 19, 22), and in the words of Paul, "in him we live, and move, and have our being" (Acts 17:28).

But, secondly, sovereignty, as the right of dominion and the fact of possession, comes to its full all-pervasive and efficient exercise in government. As such it is (1) sovereignty exercised in accordance with antecedent decree. What God decrees is infallibly determined and accomplished. "Hast thou not heard," He protests, "long ago, how I have done it, and of ancient times that I have formed it? now have I brought it to pass, that thou shouldest be to lay waste fenced cities into ruinous heaps" (II Kings 19:25). "Surely as I have thought, so shall it come to pass; and as I have purposed, so shall it stand" (Isa. 14:24). "My counsel shall stand, and I will do all my pleasure" (Isa. 26:10). In Job's words, "He is in one mind, and who can turn him? And what his soul desireth, even that he doeth. For he performeth the thing that is appointed for me: and many such things are with him" (Job 23: 13-14). "I know that thou canst do everything, and that no thought can be withholden from thee" (Job 42: 1-2). It is that "the counsel of the Lord standeth forever, the thoughts of his heart to all generations," that He "worketh all things according to the purpose of him who worketh all things after the counsel of his own will" (Ps. 33:11; Eph. 1:11).

This purposive decree is not only stated positively but also negatively. No purpose of His can be restrained, and every creature purpose that is contrary must be frustrated. "For the Lord of hosts hath purposed, and who shall disannul it? and his hand is stretched out, and who shall turn it back," (Isa. 14:27). "He maketh the devices of the people of none effect" (Ps. 33:10). "He doeth according to his will in the army of heaven, and among the inhabitants of the earth: and none can stay his hand, or say unto him, What doest thou?" (Dan. 4:35).

As Sovereignty coming to all-pervasive and efficient exercise in government, it is (2) sovereignty exercised with omnipotent and undefeatable efficiency. The mighty hand of God is the executor of His will. He is the great, the mighty, the terrible. He rideth upon the heavens and, in His excellency, on the skies. There is none who can deliver out of His hand, for He frustrateth the devices of the crafty, and the counsel of the cunning is carried headlong. He breaketh down, and it cannot be built up again. There is no wisdom nor understanding nor counsel against Him. None can stay His hand nor say unto Him, "What doest thou?" for human might is of one sort with that of the Egyptians, and they are men and not God, and their horses flesh and not spirit (Deut. 10:17; 13:26; Job 5:12-13; 12:14; Prov. 21:30; Dan. 3:35; Isa. 31:3).

It is (3) sovereignty that is all-pervasive. This all-pervasiveness rests upon His omnipresence. "Whither shall I go from thy spirit? or whither shall I flee from thy presence? If I ascend up into heaven, thou art there: if I make my bed in hell, behold, thou art there. If I take the wings of the morning, and dwell in the uttermost parts of the sea; even there shall thy hand lead me, and thy right hand shall hold me" (Ps. 139:7-10).

We may illustrate this all-pervasiveness in three of the ways in which Scripture exhibits it:

(a) It respects the events of ordinary providence. It is God who gives rain upon the earth and sends water upon the fields. He makes His sun to shine upon the evil and the good and sends rain on the just and the unjust. He clothes the grass of the field, causing the grass to grow for cattle and herb for the service of man. He feeds the birds of heaven. Not a sparrow falls to the ground without His knowledge and will. He gives us our daily bread. He gives wine that makes glad the heart of man, oil that makes his face to shine, and bread that strengthens man's heart. He crowns the years with goodness and the paths drop fatness. He even gives that which is abused and used in the service of another god. He gave grain and new wine, and the oil, and multiplied silver and gold, which they used for Baal. He makes the wind His messengers and flames of fire His ministers. The whole earth is filled with His glory. So that the pious contemplation of His working brings forth the exclamation of adoration: "O Lord, how manifold are thy works! in wisdom hast thou made them all: the earth is full of thy riches" (Job 5:10; Matt. 5:45; Ps. 104: 4, 14-24; 63:11; Hos. 2:8).

(b) It respects the disposition of all earthly authority. He alone is God of all the kingdoms of the earth. He removes kings and sets up kings, for as the Most High, He rules the kingdom of men and gives it whomsoever He will. He sets up over them even the lowest of men. It is He that gives even to ungodly men the kingdom, the power, the strength, and the glory. He overthrows the throne and strength of kingdoms (Deut. 4: 35, 39; II Kings 5:15; 9:15; Isa. 37:16; Dan. 4:17; 5:18, 21; Hag. 2:22).

The very division of the kingdom of Israel fraught with dire consequences for the true worship of Jehovah was yet a thing brought about of the Lord that He might establish His word (I Kings 12:15). "Thus saith the Lord, Ye shall not go up, nor fight against your brethren the children of Israel: return every man to his house; for this thing is from me" (I Kings 12:24). For He ordains kings for judgment and establishes them for correction, so that Assyria is the rod of His anger and the staff of His hand the divine indignation to perform the divine judgment upon Mount Zion and on Jerusalem (Hab. 1:12; Isa. 10: 5, 12).

It is not simply, then, that the powers of civil government are ordained by God to be the ministers of equity and good and peace, for the punishment of evil doers and for the praise of them that do well (Rom. 13:3; I Pet. 2:14), but it is also true that usurped and corrupt government that violates the very principles of government itself is within the government of God and fulfils His sovereign purpose. In perpetration of iniquity, they fill up the cup of divine indignation. "Wherefore it shall come to pass, that when the Lord hath performed his work upon Mount Zion and on Jerusalem, I will punish the fruit of the stout heart of the king of Assyria, and the glory of his high looks" (Isa. 10:12).

(c) It respects good and evil, so that even the sins of men come within the scope of His rule and providence. "What," asks the oppressed and the afflicted Job, bereft of flocks and herds and smitten with sore boils from the sole of his foot unto the crown, "shall we receive good at the hand of God and shall we not receive evil?" (Job 2:10). For "with God," he says again, "is wisdom and strength, he hath counsel and understanding. Behold, he breaketh down, and it cannot be built again; he shutteth up a man, and there can be no opening" (Job 12: 13-14). He forms the light and creates darkness; He makes peace and creates evil. He kills and He makes alive; He wounds and He heals (Isa. 45:7; Deut. 32:39). He "hath made all things for himself: yea, even the wicked for the day of evil" (Prov. 16:4). "Shall there be evil in a city, and the Lord hath not done it?" (Amos 3:6).

I am not in the least forgetful of the very acute problems raised by such pronouncements of Scripture. It will be the task of other speakers at this conference to deal with these in more detail, and I have no doubt but they will be ably and judiciously handled. Nevertheless it does appear necessary to the topic assigned me to affirm that the teaching of Scripture on the divine sovereignty requires us to recognize with Calvin that all events are governed by the secret counsel and directed by the present hand of God and that God's omnipotence is not the vain, idle possession of potency but the most vigilant, efficacious, and operative, "a power constantly exerted on every distinct and particular movement" (Inst. I, xvi. 3). "Whence we assert, that not only the heaven and the earth, and inanimate creatures, but also the deliberations and volitions of men, are so governed by His providence, as to be directed to the end appointed by it" (Inst. I, xvi. 8).

The problems raised come to their most acute expression in those instances where the agency of God is affirmed in connection with what is not only evil in the generic sense but evil in the specific sense of sin and wrongdoing. It appears to me that Calvin again is right when he contends that "nothing can be desired more explicit than His frequent declarations, that He blinds the minds of men, strikes them with giddiness, inebriates them with the spirit of slumber, fills them with infatuation, and hardens their hearts. These passages also many persons refer to for permission, as though, in abandoning the reprobate, God permitted them to be blinded by Satan. But that solution is too frivolous, since the Holy Spirit expressly declares that their blindness and infatuation are inflicted by the righteous judgment of God. He is said to have caused the obduracy of Pharaoh's heart, and also to have aggravated and confirmed it. Some elude the force of these expressions with a foolish cavil—that since Pharaoh himself is elsewhere said to have hardened his own heart, his own will

is stated as the cause of his obduracy; as though these
two things were at all incompatible with each other,
that man should be actuated by God, and yet at the
same time be active himself. But I retort on them their
own objection; for if *hardening* denotes a bare permission, Pharaoh cannot properly be charged with being
the cause of his own obstinacy. Now, how weak and
insipid would be such an interpretation, as though
Pharaoh only permitted himself to be hardened! Besides the Scripture cuts off all occasion of such cavils.
God says, "I will harden his heart" (Inst. I. xviii. 2).

In this connection, it is noteworthy to observe that
the prophet was commanded to go and tell the people,
"Hear ye indeed, but understand not; and see ye indeed, but perceive not. Make the heart of this people
fat, and make their ears heavy, and shut their eyes;
lest they see with their eyes, and hear with their ears,
and understand with their heart, and convert and be
healed" (Isa. 6:9-10). In the Gospels and Acts of the
Apostles, we have allusion to this part of Isaiah's
prophecy (see Matt. 13: 14-15; John 12:40; Acts 28:
26-27). In Matthew and Acts, the blinding of the eyes
is represented as the blinding on the part of the people
of their own eyes; in John it is represented as blinding
on the part of God. This variation should serve to remind us that the positive infliction on the part of God
must not be abstracted from the sinful condition of the
heart, the moral perversity and responsible action of
those who are the subjects of the divine retribution.
Paul tells us that, because men will not receive the
love of the truth that they might be saved, "for this
cause God shall send them strong delusion [working of
error], that they should believe a lie: that they all
might be damned who believed not the truth, but had

pleasure in unrighteousness" (I Thess. 2: 11-12 cf; I Kings 22: 19-23). But while we may not abstract the divine infliction from the moral situation in which those concerned find themselves, we must frankly acknowledge the reality of the divine action and the sovereignty of His agency. "Therefore hath he mercy on whom he will have mercy, and whom he will he hardeneth" (Rom. 9:18).

Perhaps most familiar to us in the matter of the divine agency as it respects evil are Acts 2:23; 4:28, where the arch-crime of human history is referred to the determinate counsel and foreknowledge of God and the treatment meted out to Jesus in the conspiracy devised against Him by Herod and Pontius Pilate and the Gentiles and the people of Israel as that which the divine hand and counsel foreordained to come to pass.

We are now attempting, only very briefly, to show some of the ways in which the witness of Scripture establishes the all-pervasiveness of the sovereignty of God. When we find this sovereignty coming to expression in the most unequivocal way even in those acts of subordinate agents where their moral responsibility is most intensely active in the perpetration of wrong, we can hardly go any farther in demonstrating the all-inclusiveness of it.

But just then we must ever remind ourselves that God contracts no defilement or criminality from such agency. He is just in all His ways and holy in all His works. While everything that occurs in God's universe finds its account, as B. B. Warfield says, "in His positive ordering and active concurrence," yet "the moral quality of the deed, considered in itself, is rooted in the moral character of the subordinate agent, acting in the circumstances and under the motives operative in each instance" (*Biblical Doctrines,* p. 20). God is not the author of sin. Sin is embraced in His decretive foreordination; it is accomplished in His providence. But it is embraced in His decree and effected in His providence in such a way as to insure that blame and guilt attach to the perpetrators of wrong and to them alone.

And again there comes to us with renewed force the significance and even preciousness of the truth that inscrutable mystery surrounds the divine working. "As thou knowest not what is the way of the spirit, nor how the bones do grow in the womb of her that is with child: even so thou knowest not the works of God who maketh all" (Eccl. 11:5). We cannot rationalize it; we cannot lay it bare so as to comprehend it. We bow in humble and intelligent ignorance and reiterate, "Canst thou by searching find out God? canst thou find out the Almighty unto perfection? It is high as heaven: what canst thou do? deeper than hell; what canst thou know? The measure thereof is longer than the earth, and broader than the sea" (Job 11: 7-9). His way is in the sea and His path in the great waters. His footsteps are not known (Ps. 77:19). Clouds and darkness are round about Him. Yet, in accordance with His holiness, Scripture never permits us to forget that justice and judgment are the habitation of His throne (Ps. 89:14).

The sovereignty of God is in a unique and peculiar way exemplified in the election to saving grace. In the Old Testament one of the most significant episodes is the revelation of the redemptive name "Jehovah." There have been various attempts to interpret the precise meaning of the name. The older view that it expresses the self-determination, the independence, in the soteric sphere, the sovereignty of God, appears to be the most acceptable and tenable. It finds the key to its meaning in the formula, "I am that I am" (Exod. 3:14). In all that God does for His people, He is determined from within Himself. Paraphrased, the formula would run, "What I am and what I shall be in relation to my people, I am and shall be in virtue of what I myself am. The rationale of my actions and relations, promises and purposes, is in myself, in my free self-determining will."

The correlate of this sovereignty in the choice and salvation of His people is the faithfulness and unchange-ableness of God. He consistently pursues the determina-tions that proceed from Himself, and so His self-consistency insures steadfastness and persistence in His covenant promises and purposes. "For I am Jehovah, I change not; therefore ye sons of Jacob are not con-sumed" (Mal. 3:6).*

Perhaps the most plausible and subtle attempt to eliminate the sovereignty of God in the election to saving grace is the interpretation that posits fore-knowledge in the diluted sense of foresight or prescience as the prius, in the order of divine thought, to predes-tination to life. The *locus classicus* in the argument is Rom. 8:29. It is contended that the foreknowledge spoken of is the divine foresight of faith, or, more comprehensively, the divine foresight of the fulfilment on the part of men of the conditions of salvation. Those whom He foreknew, therefore, are those whom He fore-saw as certain to fulfill the conditions of salvation.

It is thought that this removes the reason for the dis-

---

* Cf. Oehler, **Old Testament Theology**, Eng. trans., vol. I, pp. 139f, Geerhardus Vos, **Lectures on the Theology of the Old Testament,** ch. VIII

crimination that exists among men in the matter of salvation from the sovereign discrimination and fore-ordination on the part of God to the sovereign volition on the part of man. Of the Pelagian or Arminian conception of the origin of faith, it must be understood that it makes no real difference that the matter concerns the eternal decree of God. The question really is, what is the crucial and determining factor in predestination to life? Is it a sovereign act on the part of God or is it an activity or exercise of will on the part of man? Once the predestinating decree of God is made contingent upon the divine foresight of an autonomous action or decision on the part of man, then it is that action on the part of man that accounts for discriminating foreordination on the part of God. And so the sovereignty of God in the election to life is eliminated at the crucial point. Predestination is made to rest upon a condition resident in, or fulfilled by, man.

If, for the sake of argument, we were to adopt this diluted interpretation of the verb "foreknow" in Rom. 8:29, we are not to readily conclude that what we call the particularistic exegesis would have to be abandoned and the absolute sovereignty of God in the matter of election to life be eliminated. If we say that the meaning of the verb "foreknow" in Rom. 8:29 is "whom He foresaw as believing and persevering," we are not to think that we have ended the matter, for we are compelled to ask the further question: Whence this faith which God foresees?

The answer that Scripture itself affords is that faith itself is the gift of God, not of course gift in some mechanical sense, but gift in the sense of being graciously wrought in men by the operation and illumination of the Spirit (see e.g., John 3: 3-8; 6: 44, 45, 65;

Eph. 2:8; Phil. 1:21). Since faith is thus given to some and not to others, and given to those who are equally unworthy with those to whom it is not given, the ultimate reason is that God is pleased thus to operate in some and not in others. The divine foresight of faith, therefore, would presuppose an antecedent decree on the part of God to work this faith in some and not in others. The foresight of faith would have as its logical prius the sovereign determination to give faith to them. And so even foresight would, on a Biblical conception of the origin of faith, throw us back on the sovereign determination of God.

This exegesis, however, though really providing no escape from the sovereignty of God in the decree of salvation, is nevertheless not to be favored, and that for the following reasons:

(1) It is extremely unlikely that Paul, in tracing our salvation to its source in the mind and will of God, would have omitted reference to the originative decree, namely, the decree to work faith.

(2) According to the teaching of Scripture in general and Paul in particular, faith is included in, or associated with, *klesis,* and *klesis* is in this very passage made the consequence of foreknowledge and predestination. It cannot be both the condition of predestination and the consequence of it.

This consideration is confirmed by verse 28: "All things work together for good to them that love God, to those who are the called according to his purpose." If called according to His purpose, the purpose is antecedent to the calling, and if faith is embodied in or associated with calling, the purpose itself cannot be conditioned upon faith.

(3) This exegesis is in conflict with what is said to

be the end of predestination—conformity to the image
of His Son. Conformity of this kind is surely meant to
include every phase of likeness to Christ. Conformity
to the image of the Son, no doubt, points to the ultimate
perfection to which the elect will attain. If so, then the
whole process by which that conformity is secured and
realized must be in subordination to this end. In other
words, the end is surely prior in the order of thought
to the process by which it is to be achieved. But the
process by which the end is to be achieved includes faith
and perseverance. Faith cannot then be the logical antecedent of predestination; it is rather that predestination
is the logical antecedent of faith, even of faith as fore-
seen by God in His eternal counsel. That is just saying
that faith is consequent, in the order of divine thought,
upon the destined end of conformity to the image of the
Son. But the antecedent of predestination faith would
have to be if foreknowledge is the foreknowledge of
faith.

Faith, therefore, is two removes in the order of
divine thought from foreknowledge, and two removes
posterior, not prior, two removes in the order of consequence, not of causation.

(4) This line of interpretation is in accord with
Paul's teaching elsewhere and particularly in that one
passage which more than any other expands the very
subject in debate. It is Eph. 1:4.

(a) Paul there affirms that God chose us in Christ
"before the foundation of the world, that we should be
holy and without blame before Him in love: having
predestinated us unto adoption of children by Jesus
Christ to Himself." The elect are chosen to holiness;
in the divine love, they are predestinated to adoption.

(b) This election and predestination are according

to the good pleasure of His will and according to the purpose of Him who worketh all things according to the purpose of His own will. Paul, it is to be noted, piles up expressions almost to the point of what might be, on superficial reading, considered redundancy, in order to emphasize the sovereign determination of the divine will and purpose: *"proisthéntes katà prôthesin toū tâ pânta énergountos katà tēn boulēn toū theiámatos autoū."* To find the determining factor in this predestination in a human decision would be to wreck the whole intent of Paul's eloquent multiplication of terms.

(c) The choice in Christ and the consequent union with Him is the antecedent or foundation of all the blessings bestowed. It is in the Beloved we were abundantly favored with grace (vs. 6); it is in Him we have the redemption, the forgiveness of sins according to the riches of His grace (vs. 7); the making known of the mystery of His will was purposed in Christ (vs. 9); it is in Him that all things in heaven and earth will be summed up (vs. 10): it is in Him we are called (vs. 11); it is in Him that the Ephesians, when they had heard the word of truth and believed, were sealed with the Holy Spirit of promise (vss. 13, 14). It is obvious that the very exercise of grace, believing and persevering grace, is grace exercised in the sphere and on the basis of union with Christ, and so the union with Christ which has its genesis in the choice of Christ before the foundation of the world, must be regarded as the prius and basis of that grace rather than, by way of prescience, its conditioning cause.

If this exegesis, which takes the verb "foreknow" in the diluted sense of prescience, is not acceptable, what then, we may ask, is the meaning of foreknowledge? The answer, given repeatedly by the ablest commentators, is not difficult to find. The words *yādhà* in Hebrew and *ginōskō* in Greek are used quite frequently in a pregnant sense, that is, with a fuller meaning than that of merely perceiving or taking cognizance of a fact. It often means to "take note of," to "set regard upon," to "know with peculiar interest, delight, affection, and even action." Indeed, it is the practical synonym of "to love" or "set affection upon." "The compound *proginōskō*," as Sanday observes, "throws back this 'taking note' from the historic act in time to the eternal counsel which it expresses and executes" (Comm., *in loco*). So that we should paraphrase by saying, "Those whom He loved beforehand."

This pregnant meaning of the word is in accord with contextual considerations. In every other link of this "golden chain of salvation," as it has been called, it is a divine activity that is spoken of. God is intensely active in every other step. It is God Who predestinates; it is God Who calls; it is God Who justifies; it is God Who glorifies. It would be out of accord with this emphasis, a weakening at the point that can least afford it, to make the originative act of God less active and determinative. The notion of foresight has distinctly less of the active and distinctly more of the passive than the divinely nonergistic emphasis of the whole passage appears to require. It is not a foresight of difference but a foreknowledge that makes difference to exist. It does not simply recognize existence; it determines existence. It expresses the volitional determinative counsel of God with reference to those who are the objects of it. It is sovereign distinguishing love.

If this is the meaning, the question may well be

asked: What is the difference between foreknowledge and predestination in the text concerned? For, after all, some distinction there must be.

The distinction is simple and significant. Foreknowledge is the setting of loving and knowing affection upon those concerned. It concentrates attention upon the love of God. But it does not of itself intimate the specific destiny to which the objects of love are appointed. That, in turn, predestination precisely does. It reveals to us the high and blessed destiny to which the objects of His distinguishing and peculiar love are assigned. And it reveals, in so doing, the greatness of His love. It is love of such a sort that it assigns them to conformity to the image of Him Who is the eternal and only-begotten Son.

When we ask the reason for the love that foreknowledge intimates and the greatness and security of which predestination expresses, we are uniquely confronted with the grandeur of the divine sovereignty. It is love that is according to the counsel of the divine will. The reason is enveloped in the mystery of His good pleasure. We are face to face with an ultimate of divine revelation and, therefore, an ultimate of human thought. This love is not something that we can rationalize or analyze. We are in its presence, as nowhere else, overwhelmed with a sense of the divine sovereignty. We are struck with amazement. It is amazing, inexplicable love. But to faith it is a reality that constrains the deepest and highest adoration. It is love, the praise of which eternity will not exhaust. "Herein is love, not that we loved God, but that he loved us, and sent his Son to be the propitiation for our sins" (I John 4:10). "O the depth of the riches both of the wisdom and knowledge of

God! how unsearchable are his judgments, and his ways past finding out! For who hath known the mind of the Lord? or who hath been his counsellor? or who hath first given to him, and it shall be recompensed unto him again? For of him, and through him, and to him, are all things: to whom be glory forever. Amen" (Rom. 11: 33-36).

A DOGMATIC STUDY

THE REV. PRINCIPAL JOHN MACLEOD, D.D.

THE LORD is the true God and an everlasting King. He is the Maker of all things, and as such He is their Lord. They are His work which He has made for Himself. They belong to His lordship, or kingdom. They owe their being to His will and word. In the wide range of derived or created being, which all belongs to His nature and is embraced in His decree, there is not only the region of the inanimate, or the merely sentient; there is that also of animate and intelligent or spiritual being, which was made to hold fellowship with Him from Whom it has come. Angels that excel in strength belong to this realm. We also, who are of an order that was made a little lower than they, belong to it as well. And we have a closer and more personal concern with the truth that bears on our race and on ourselves than we have with what holds good of another, albeit a higher rank of being than our own.

Each of us as well as the whole race to which we belong are subject to the scepter of the blessed and only Potentate, the King of kings and Lord of lords. Made in His likeness and for His glory, we should have our blessedness in Him. In regard to this, we are as much dependent on the Lord for our blessedness as we are for our very being; and this we are not only as creatures, as our first father was before the Fall, but very specially do we depend on Him for restored blessedness as creatures that have sinned. Sinners have earned the wrath and curse of God, and if they are to be freed from His righteous wrath, it can be only as the outcome of His holy will in gracious intervention. The evil thing from which we need to be set free takes the shape of war with God. The very mind, or thinking, of man as fallen is enmity against Him. It is not subject to His law neither indeed can be, and so long as the reign of this evil principle remains unbroken, those who are under its sway cannot please God. They have their wicked quarrel with Him; and cherishing the thought of rebels, they are not willing to own Him as King or to give Him the glory of His kingly supremacy. They will not submit to the revelation of His will in law as the rule of their obedience. Their quarrel with His royal rights comes out directly in their self-will, which casts off His yoke. They would still, like their first father, be a god to themselves. And they dare to set up what falls in with their own pleasure against what He is pleased to make known as His preceptive will. The intimation of His preceptive will is one of the ways in which the great King makes it known that He is King. Those who would dethrone or ignore Him by ruling His authority out of their lives set at nought His will. They say in effect that their tongues are their own. Who is Lord over them? Thus the virus that was injected into the race by the tempter at the first is still at work and men will not yield to the claims of God as He calls for a loyal response in obedience at the hand of a race that He made to be His subjects and His servants.

This is one side of God's sovereignty; and it is often overlooked and forgotten when we speak of the matter. And yet when our attention is drawn to it, we see at once how it belongs to His kingly glory that it should be His revealed will that ought to guide the outgoings of our soul in the varied obediences of life. As a rule, among Christian people there is an acknowledgment of this kingship, even though the best have reason to mourn over how far they have come short of the love and the loyalty that should be theirs in their answer to the righteous claims of God. We see, however, that even on this side in regard to the obedience due to his Maker by man as fallen, there is a disposition shown by many to reduce the claim that God makes at the hand of the sinner as though the sinful disability that man has brought upon himself availed to exempt him from some share of the full task of duty for which his Maker calls. This perversion of truth may take more forms than one.

The plea may be put forward that man is responsible for only what is within reach and compass of his present power. When this ground is taken, we see how those who adopt it as their starting point and yet acknowledge the right of God to call for repentance and faith stand out for seriously weakened and watered down doctrine of the disastrous results of the Fall on the race of mankind. And they reason that when men are called upon to repent and believe the gospel, they must have some reserve of power still inherent in their nature, which lays a rational ground for asking such obedience from them! Along this line lies Pelagianism, with its diluted varieties and modifications in Semi-Pelagian Synergism and Arminianism. Those who espouse this kind of teaching reason from "I must" to "I can." They infer that there is power where there is duty. The pride of unbroken and unhumbled human nature comes out in the Kantian ethic that deduces "I can" from "I ought." It forgets that the disability that comes in the train of sin does not take away from God the right to ask for the love and the service to yield which He made us in His likeness at the first. To take this away from Him would be as much as to say that sin has so far reached its goal as to spoil our Maker of His right to call for full and unabated obedience at the hand of men who have fallen away from Him. Now, the teaching that finds a place for such a leaven joins issue with the truth that the Lord is King. It quarrels with the rightful authority that belongs to Him as Maker and Sovereign.

This, however, is not all. If there are left-hand defections, there are right-hand extremes, for among those who own the truth of the spiritual bankruptcy of a fallen race, there are some who reason that because man as a sinner is unable until he is born again to repent or to believe the gospel, he is not called upon to do either and it would not be reasonable that he should be called upon to yield such obedience. It is said to be a mockery of his misery or it is a suggestion that he is not so lost as not to be able to make his way back to God. Now, it is neither the one thing nor the other. It is not a mockery of the wretchedness of the sinner, which on the part of his fellow in sin would be a very heartless thing. It is the way that God Himself takes in His Word in dealing with the many who are called outwardly, as many of whom hear and heed not. For many are called, while few are chosen. He bids men make, then, a new heart, and this is fitted when they try to comply with the Word and find how wretchedly they fail, to let them see the wickedness and stubbornness of hearts that will neither tremble nor obey. And at the same time, it is fitted to produce the conviction that such is the grip of spiritual death that nothing else can loosen it than the new birth from above, which gives life to the dead. Such a method conveys no suggestion that the thing that a man ought to do he can do. He ought to do it, and he has to learn that what he ought to do he cannot do and that this is the pit of hopeless ruin into which his sin has plunged him. It is a bitter thing to learn this truth, but it is a wholesome truth to learn. It is not we who are only called upon to echo His word, but God Himself that bids the impenitent repent, the unbelieving believe, and the dead to do what only the living can do. In doing all this, God is within His own right, and He vindicates the wisdom of the way that He is pleased to take when He brings on sinners guilty in the court of conscience and makes them feel that they are quite consciously impotent by reason of the dominion of death over their nature. When He does this, He teaches the truth of spiritual death in the hard school of a living experience. This is something more than acquaintance with doctrinal notions. God convinces those whom He thus teaches that they must depend on Him as God, Who quickeneth the dead, Who alone can give effect to His own word of truth, and Who alone can burst the bonds that lie on the person and his powers over which the apathy of death holds its sway. The subjects of this teaching can speak of things whose truth they have been made to feel.

That our race should be in such a sad plight is a mystery that we are bound to recognize to be one that we cannot fathom and it is folly on our part to try to explain it away by our proud and empty reasoning. In his pride, man the culprit would take as his own the seat of the Judge and arraign his Judge to his bar as though the role of Judge and culprit were reversed. He forgets that He with Whom he has to do is one that giveth not account of His matters and is not amenable to the judgment of the creatures that owe their very being to His kingly fiat. Well would it become each of us in things of this kind to hearken to the voice that spoke of old at the bush: "Take off thy shoes from off thy feet for the place whereon thou standest is holy ground."

The truth of Scripture has a catholicity of its own, an all-round fulness and symmetry that man with his nibbling cavils would mar and mutilate. The whole truth as to man's awful ruin is to be held and taught subject to no abatement, and the full tale of God's un-abridged rights and claims is at the same time to be held and taught along with it. And so the twofold truth that man ought to obey and yet he cannot is to be maintained in its integrity. There is a lofty superiority to the whittling schemes of man in how the Word of God sets forth both sides of this truth, doing full justice to each alike. In this respect our Reformed Faith in its fullest confession and expression as it sets forth standard Reformed teaching in such symbolic documents as the "Canons of Dort" and "The Westminster Confession of Faith" is a true echo of the doctrine of the Word, which these notable symbols undertook to declare and to defend. The sacred rights of law as an utterance of the holy will of God are guarded and at the same time unmistakable witness is borne to the need that there is for the saving operation of God, so that man may be restored to the likeness he has lost. He will thus only be enabled to answer the end of his being when he answers the end of his calling in wearing the yoke of his redeeming Lord. We are thus brought up to face the question of what effects this gracious result. And this is the other aspect of sovereignty which is to be seen not in the authoritative proclamation of the preceptive will of God, the Lawgiver and King, but in His decisive will as He appoints things to be in His external decree.

This second aspect of His sovereignty of which we are now to speak is what is oftenest indicated by the word when it is used of God. Stress is laid in historical and dogmatic discussions on the disposal of all things according to the purpose of God as that is wrought out in the field of universal providence. At times, the word "predestination" may be used in a narrower and at other times in a wider sense. The stress of thought may be laid on the decree that bears in electing grace on the destiny of the people of God and its twin decree that bears on the appointed destiny of those that He is pleased to pass over and to ordain to wrath and to dishonor as the reward of their sin. In the wider sense of predestination, it covers all events, so that God is seen to have preordained whatsoever comes to pass, and the regularity of natural law is due to His appointment as to the necessary working of second causes according to the nature that He has bestowed upon them and their consequent appropriate working. In the course of His government in providence, He works out what He has decreed so that these second or subordinate causes have their field of proper operation or activity according to the nature of each. Thus events that are contingent fall out contingently, and what is necessary has its own necessity. In the range of this latter category, paradoxical as it may sound, it is necessary that the functioning of the created will should be free so that if it is to be exercised at all there is a needs be that it should be free. Thus rational freedom and necessity are found to conspire sweetly in the production of the actions of free agents. Here then is a necessity that has in its nature nothing of the character of a compelling force to overbear rational freedom. So the predestination of God does not clash with the responsible freedom with which He has endowed accountable creatures whom He has put under law and laid under obligation to honor Him by obeying it.

When a free agent in the exercise of his personal natural spontaneity takes a course of action it was certain beforehand that he would take such a course and should be naturally free in doing so. For God, Who appointed before that such a course should be taken, in doing so, appointed that it should be taken by a free agent in the natural exercise of his proper freedom. Such an appointment does not mar the freedom of the agent or his responsibility for his act. So far is this from being the case, that it made sure that without any compulsion the action should take place and that it should be free when it takes place. An appointment of this kind lays no kind of blind or brute necessity upon a free agent that interferes with his native spontaneous freedom or binds the agent hand and foot to be or to do anything else than he sees fit to choose for himself. Thus the sovereignty of God in His purpose of predestination or preordination is a guarantee beforehand that when the time and place come for rational accountable action such action shall be taken in the full range of its rationality and responsibility. That God has appointed that a thing should be free is what secures and makes certain that it shall be so. It makes it certain beforehand: and this certainty does not come in conflict with the truth of the freedom of the willing agent when he in due course wills to act and acts as he has willed. It is a mere bugbear that is conjured up when men say that the predestination of God with its attendant certainty prohibits the free eventuation of the acts of responsible agents. God has appointed that responsible action should be that of free agents in the exercise of their choice as it commends itself to them and as they shall answer for it.

To say that the purpose beforehand to make a being endowed with rational freedom is inconsistent with the true freedom of that being when made is as much as to say that no truly free and accountable creature can exist; for to be such a free creature is only the thought of the Creator Who designed to make such a being. The creature will is free as it chooses what the person sees to be good for choice. It was made to be free, and the purpose to make it was a purpose to make it what it was meant to be. There is thus no quarrel between man's creation as a morally free being and his freedom and there is no more of a quarrel between that freedom and God's purpose to make beings endowed with such a freedom. Man made in the likeness and for the service of his Maker was not meant to be a mere piece of automatic mechanism grinding out irresponsible thought and desire and action. In his own sphere, he was meant to be an originating center of spontaneous and voluntary acts and of an activity that is a reflection on the plane of created life and being of the supreme and controlling activity of the will of God, our Maker. Thus the sovereign counsel of God has effect given to it, and yet it not only does not impinge upon the entire freedom of the will of free agents but it has in its certainty of execution the pledge that each responsible creature of His hand shall have all the freedom that is needed for the responsibility for which He has given it being. There is then a perfect harmony between the will of a sovereign God, the blessed and only Potentate, as effectual and controlling and transcendent, and the will or freedom of His responsible creatures who take the way that commends itself to their choice. At one and the same time, the will of God is sovereign and supreme and the will of man is naturally and morally free. Neither has a real quarrel with the other though the perverse and rebel will of fallen man has its steady quarrel from day to day with the preceptive will of the Holy Sovereign of heaven and earth. The exercise of the will of the creature leaves him open to the account that he has to give in. His responsibility is unimpaired. And it is altogether an oblique view that is taken of the supreme control and certainty of God's decretive will when it is shown as if it were in conflict with the fundamental and undeniable truth that we as a race are amenable to the judgment in righteousness of the great King, eternal, immortal, and invisible.

There is no conflict at this point. In a word, we may say that as surely as God is sovereign, man is free, and as surely as man is free, God is sovereign. In the sovereignty that belongs to Him, He so controls the thoughts and devices and volitions of His creatures as to carry out through their free and responsible activity what He has Himself designed. His supremacy sets bounds to the activity of His creatures so that at the very time and in the very thing in which they please themselves they are giving effect to His transcendent design. And His is so even should it be the thought of their heart that they are bent on frustrating His counsel by doing their own will or pleasure. When this self-will reaches its highest, His controlling hand is high above it.

There is of course an important distinction in the meaning we put upon the word "free" when we apply it to the ordinary rational choice and activity of every man in every-day life, which marks it out from the sense that attaches to it when we deny the spiritual freedom in things spiritual to those only whose spiritual freedom of will has been given back to them by the touch of renewing grace. On such subjects as fall to be discussed in this connection, we cannot be too careful as to the precise sense in which we and others use the words that are the coinage or currency of thought. It is the failure to define our terms and to adhere to the definition made and accepted that brings in the confusion that is found so often in the handling of topics in which ambiguity lurks at every corner owing to the various shades of meaning that belong to the same word as they are used in the dialect of various schools of thought. It is one of the benefits that issue from dogmatic or theological conflict that the combatants are forced by the necessity of the case to clear their ground and to use their terms with a respectable amount of self-consistency. In the field of philosophy, we may ascribe to man a freedom that in the contiguous field of theology we may deny to him. When we understand the terms that we use in these neighboring realms of thought, we see that it is quite consistent to ascribe to man as a moral agent an inalienable freedom, while in regard to spiritual service to God, his Maker, we deny to him as fallen the true and holy freedom which was his glory in his unfallen state. Then to do God's will was man's true delight; and such delight he cannot again have in the will and law of God until that law is written on the fleshly tablets of a new heart as the promise of the New Covenant has been made good to him.

By the misuse of his natural freedom of will, man lost both himself and his true freedom of will. He is thus without the power to yield the homage of a loyal heart to the will of God. This being so, he is often spoken of as if he were destitute of freedom of will, in which usage "power" and "freedom" are almost convertible or interchangeable terms. He is in bondage as fallen to the deformity of his nature so as not to be able to choose or to will as he should. This inability is bondage, which is the negation of freedom. Yet as he is in possession of spontaneity of action and makes his own choice, he has a natural freedom that is enough to leave him responsible for the choice that he makes and the course that he takes.

It is in regard to the bondage of the will to sin that, in the field of history, discussion took place in the Pelagian controversy. The Pelagians denied the truth of the teaching of the orthodox, which laid stress on the spiritual bondage of man as a fallen being. In connection with this denial, they had their quarrel with the sovereign will of God in regard to the dispensation of His grace; and this quarrel has passed on along the line of their avowed successors, such for instance as the Socinians. In a modified form, we find the Semi-Pelagian strain taking up this teaching and so quarreling with the free and absolute sovereignty of God's will in the distribution of His saving favor and salvation. This holds of the earlier and later Semi-Pelagians, so that the Arminians both of the early seventeenth century and of the Methodist movement join hands with the first representatives of their tendency in raising opposition to the freedom and sovereignty of the love and will of God in the choice of a people who shall reap the good of His thoughts of saving love. The criticism that Pelagianism in its several varieties makes on the truth of the sovereignty of grace is rooted in the unhumbled and self-righteous thoughts of men who fail to see that they are indeed sinners or who have no just or serious sense of the evil of sin and of the righteousness of the doom that is out against it and that lies upon the sinner because of it. An uncircumcised heart is its source.

The objections that an Apostle had to face recur down the ages. Man will still ask "Who has resisted His will?" so that they have to be told that it does not belong to the thing that is made to say to its Maker, "Why hast thou made me thus?" They need to be told that God, our Maker, is our Lord and King, being all that He is and all that the ideal Lord and King must be. If to be an ideal king among men one must be wise and just and true and good, these things raised to the height of full perfection and bearing the stamp of unending immutability belong to the Sovereign of heaven and earth. If a king to be a king indeed must be good, He is good. There is none good but one; that is God. If he must be true, He is true. If he must be just, He is just. If he must be wise, He is wise. If he must be mighty, He is mighty. And in all these things He is infinite, eternal, and unchangeable, while over and above His wisdom, power, justice, goodness, and truth, He is as perfect in the beauty of His holiness as He is in all His other attributes. Of such an One, it is not to be thought that He should not be trusted even in the dark. Nor should we dare to think of Him and of His ways that these are not in Him and in them things that

cannot be searched out. It is not for us to dream of
calling such an One to our bar to answer for His ways
as though He were subject to our judgment, while as a
matter of fact we are subject to His judgment and not
He to ours. Thus in the infinitude of His being, there
are depths that no plumb-line of ours can fathom, so
that it is sheer presumption on the side of man to take
the measuring rod of his own creature mind to measure
the ways and thoughts of One whose judgments are unsearchable and Whose ways are past finding out. In
these things, it is our true wisdom to be clad with lowli-
ness of mind, for we are dealing with things that are
so high above us that we cannot order our speech by
reason of darkness. When such wisdom is shown as
keeps man within his proper bonds, he will sit as a
little child at the footstool of God as He speaks in His
Word and he will say, "I will hear what the Lord will
speak." It is to souls of such gracious docility that
these things of the kingdom are made known which are
hid from the wise and prudent. They are of such a
temper because they have been born from above, and
this new birth is the outflow and the token of the high
Sovereign distinguishing love of Him Who in His counsel of peace and purpose of love set them apart from
everlasting to be His own.

It is a fruit of God's kingly choice that comes out
in the efficacious, saving work of the Holy Ghost. For
there is a bond that binds into one scheme or system
the truths of the doctrines of grace. These doctrines
are parts of one whole. With God's sovereign choice,
goes hand in hand His kingly provision and destination
of the redeeming work of His Son in the effectual working of His gracious call as He quickens His called ones
to newness of life. It is this working that begets faith;

and the conversion or the turning of the sinner to God is the result of the renewing of his will, which has been wrought by the effectual call. The newness of life thus given is seen in an abiding inclination of the called ones to obedience, so that the renewal of their will prompts them willingly to abide in Him to whom they have betaken themselves, and thus they persevere in the faith and in new obedience. This willing abiding in the Vine or in the City of Refuge, tells of the operation in real grace of the love that in the purpose of grace sets apart its objects to be vessels prepared unto glory. That which is born of the Spirit is spirit, so that the new-born have in them that which cleaves to the Lord and His good ways. The outflow of sovereign choice in electing love is found in the reality of the new life of the regenerate which, beginning at their call, will reach its crown of completion in the achieved perfection of the subjects of grace here and in the kingdom of glory hereafter.

Before the Pelagian controversy, what was in substance the system that called forth the witness of Augustine to the doctrines of grace had been taught by men such as Clement of Alexandria and other church teachers in whose case their philosophy gave law to their theology. That philosophy had at its heart a pagan strain. Along with these earlier philosophic theologians, we may take the general strain of the teachers of the Greek Church, who were not given to an Augustinian type of teaching. The influence of Augustine as one of the recognized and accepted doctors of the church told on the western churches in such a succession as we find in the names of outstanding teachers such as Anselm and Bernard, far in Aquinas, so that there was a definite Augustinian tradition which gave the evangelical element to the mixed teaching of the Middle Ages. A Gottschalk might be condemned and a Semi-Pelagian strain might prevail among the Scotists and the Franciscans of pre-Reformation days. Yet so great was the authority that was recognized as belonging to Augustine that when the threads of Medieval Scholasticism were woven into one fabric at Trent, the Council aimed at avoiding any finding that would come into conflict with the teaching of the great Bishop of Hippo, while with equal care it sought to shun any form of words that would condemn the semi-Pelagianism that was rampant in the current teaching of the church and the schools. So intellectual acrobats went through their gymnastic exercises of balancing themselves on the tight rope by coming to non-committal findings that kept their doctrine from being too definite on the one side or the other of debated questions that were open in the schools.

The Augustinian strain that came out in Jansenius and Bajus was a more emphatic utterance of the doctrine of grace than the teaching that found acceptance in Lutheran circles from the latter days of Melanchthon's life onward or in the beginning of the Arminian movement in the Reformed churches. The earlier stage of the Reformation showed the leading teachers of the Protestant world to be very much at one as to the gratuitous character of the gospel of salvation. Their movement was indeed a resurgence of the teaching of the Doctor of Grace. This marked them out to begin with from the half-way men of the Humanistic Reform. In the main features of their teaching, the first Reformers were of one mind as to the gracious character of salvation. They were also at one with the teaching of the line of the Augustinian witnesses of earlier days except that in the sphere of relative grace they made a great advance in setting forth the truth as taught by the Apostles in regard to the free justification by faith of the believing sinner. This advance made clear the distinction between grace as it renews the nature and grace as it rectifies the standing of those to whom it is shown. As things came about, the defense of the truly gratuitous character of the provision of the gospel fell to be made by the Reformed as distinct from the Lutheran churches. They were in the Augustinian tradition on the subject.

In England, the first uprising of a type of teaching that came in conflict with the true Reformed Confession was firmly repressed and the Lambeth Articles made plain to the world the strict Reformed orthodoxy of the leaders of the Anglican Communion in the latter days of Queen Elizabeth. It was not then to be wondered at that the representatives of England at the Synod of Dort should join in the condemnation of Arminianism in the profession of the Reformed Faith in regard to the decree of God which recognizes His holy sovereignty in the dispensing of His saving favor.

The findings of the renowned ecumenical Synod of the Reformed Churches set forth this faith as it was held in the great theological age which followed the Reformation itself when the divines of western Protestant Europe were thoroughly at home in the kind of questions that were at issue between their churches and Rome and in particular were alive to the meaning of the marked Semi-Pelagian teaching of their Jesuit opponents, who were the foremost champions of the Papacy as they were the keenest critics of the doctrine of the Reformers. It was no convention of novices or of weaklings that met at Dort in 1618. They had among their leaders and counselors some of the foremost divines of their day, and the conclusions at which they arrived in the avowal of their faith and in the condemnation of error were not hastily reached. They were the ripe decisions of a generation of theologians who were at home in their subject, expert in wielding their weapons, and temperate and restrained in the terms in which they set forth their judgment. Coming as they did in point of time after the National Confessions and Catechisms of the Reformed Churches except the documents of the Westminster Assembly, they with these documents of British origin are the culminating exhibition of our common Reformed Faith when it was called upon to unfold its inmost genius and essence in self-defense against the revived Semi-Pelagianism of the early Arminians. Their statements on these subjects put in short compass the dogmatic teaching of our churches. Thus the Canons of Dort say: "Art. I. When all men sinned in Adam and became exposed to curse and eternal death God would have done wrong to no one if He had decided to leave the whole human race in sin and curse and condemn it because of sin. . . . Art. II. But in this was manifested the love of God that He sent His only begotten Son into the world that every one that believes in Him should not perish but have eternal life. Art. III. That men, however, may be led to faith God in His clemency sends heralds of this most joyful message to whom He will and when He will by whose ministry men are called to repentance and faith in Christ crucified. . . . Art. IV. Over those who do not believe this gospel the wrath of God abides. But those who receive it and with a true and living faith embrace Jesus the Saviour are through Him set free from the wrath of God and destruction and have granted to them eternal life. . . . Art. V. The cause, or fault, of this unbelief as of all other sins is in no wise in God, but in man. But faith in Jesus Christ, and salvation through Him, is the free gift of God. . . . Art. VI. Now that in time God bestows faith on some and not on others is a thing that proceeds from His eternal decree . . . according to which decree He graciously softens the hearts of the elect however hard they be and binds them to believing while by His just judgment He leaves the non-elect to their own wickedness and hardness. And here in particular a deep distinction opens itself up to us, one that is at the same time merciful and righteous, between men that are equally lost or we may call it the decree of election and reprobation revealed in the Word of God. . . . Art. VII. Now election is the unchangeable purpose of God, by which before the foundations of the world were laid, according to the most free pleasure of His will, and of His mere grace, out of all mankind, fallen by their own fault from their first integrity into sin and destruction, He has chosen a definite number of certain men neither better nor more worthy than others but lying in common misery with others to redemption in Christ, whom He from eternity appointed the Mediator and Head of all the elect, and foundation of salvation. And so He deemed to give them to Him to be saved, and by His Word and Spirit effectually to call and draw them to a communion with Him; that is, to give them a true faith in Him to justify, sanctify, and finally glorify them, being powerfully kept in the communion of His Son to the showing forth of His mercy and the praise of the riches of His glorious grace. . . . Art. IX. This same election was made not upon foresight of faith, and the obedience of faith, holiness or any other good quality and disposition, as a cause or condition before required in man to be chosen; but unto faith, and the

obedience of faith, holiness, etc. And therefore election
is the foundation of all saving good, from which faith,
holiness [and the other gifts of salvation], lastly, everlasting life itself do flow as its fruits and effects. . . .
Art. X. The true cause of this free election is the good
pleasure of God; not consisting herein, that, from among
all possible means, He chose some certain qualities or
actions of men as a condition of salvation; but herein
that out of the common crowd of sinners He summoned
to Himself for His special possession certain persons. . . .
Art. XI. And as God Himself is most wise, unchangeable, omniscient and omnipotent, as the election made
by Him can neither be interrupted nor changed nor
recalled or disannulled nor can the elect be cast away
nor their number diminished."

This teaching is but an exposition or expansion of the
teaching of the Belgic Confession and what it has to say
on the subject. So in brief compass the Second Helvetic
Confession which found so wide an acceptance in the
Reformed Churches says: "God hath from the beginning
freely and of His grace without any respect of men
predestinated or elected the saints whom He will save in
Christ." So also we find in the Irish Articles which
passed through the hands of James Ussher such words
as these: "By the same eternal counsel, God hath predestinated some unto life, and reprobated some unto
death, of both which there is a certain number known
only to God, which can neither be increased nor diminished." This choice these articles go on to attribute
only to the good pleasure of God Himself. There is
no question as to the agreement of the Westminster
documents with a common consensus of the Reformed
Churches as they deal with this matter of divine
sovereignty and predestination.

AND THE BARTHIANS

The Rev. Prof. D. Kromminga

I AM GRATEFUL for the able presentation, in the two
preceding papers read at this conference, of the Biblical
basis and the systematic development of the doctrine
of God's sovereignty, so that I can presuppose what was
there stated. I wish also to record my appreciation of
the fact that the subject on which I am to speak has
just now been reformulated as being the question of
the relationship which Karl Barth sustains to Calvinism,
since this relieves me of the impossible task of giving
in the time at my disposal a somewhat complete presentation of the Barthian conception of God's sovereignty. It is Barth's great and pervasive emphasis on
the sovereignty of God that quite frequently leads people to class him as a Calvinist, and, if the mere presence
and prominence of a doctrine of God's sovereignty
makes the author of a theological system of thought a
Calvinist, then Karl Barth must be so classified. However, his utterances on the subject are of a nature that
makes it imperative that he should be interrogated on a
number of points before that classification is accepted.
I wish to call your attention to eleven such points.

1. *Sovereignty as a Relation or an Attribute*

Calvinists can show considerable appreciation for the Barthian insistence on the paradoxical nature of the truth and on the need of the dialectical method in order to do justice to this nature of the truth as long as this insistence can be viewed as tactical rather than essential with the Barthians and as long as they will recognize a synthesis of the apparent antitheses in God. It has been quite properly remarked at this conference that one weakness of our time is its tendency to single-track thinking, and that we need to cultivate double-track thinking. Perhaps we should speak of multiple-track thinking. A very common illustration of our need of such thinking, and one that lies quite close to the point I am now dealing with, is afforded by the problem of the relationship of the divine sovereignty and human responsibility, which two in speculative thought are always threatening to devour one another.

However, this observation must now be applied to something that lies behind the problem of the relationship between God's sovereignty and man's responsibility. The question I have in mind is whether God's sovereignty is a relation in which God stands or an attribute of His being. I am glad that at this conference God's sovereignty has unhesitatingly been qualified as a relation, since I am convinced that such a conception of it ought to be our starting-point, whatever qualifications it may then be needful to add. Nevertheless, I cannot forget the examination at our seminary which once upon a time I attended and at which a candidate unhesitatingly classified God's lordship with His attributes, and there seemed to be no one to challenge him. It would seem that, when we insist God's lordship is a relation, we must not forget that there is another side to the matter and that certain important qualifications must indeed be added.

A relation always presupposes not one but at least two entities between which it obtains. When we think of the relationship between God and the world, we must guard against conceiving of these two as more or less equally ultimate, which would strip the absoluteness from God's sovereignty over the world and reduce it to something relative at best. The point in speculation at which the ultimacy of God and the world are conceived of as equal is the point at which the sovereignty disappears completely from His relation to the world. Sovereignty is precisely a term employed to indicate that God and the world are not equal, and it is described as absolute in order to bring out its harmony with the fact that we have only one ultimate, viz., God. On the other hand, to carry God's lordship back into His very being and essence drives us into the direction of seeing the world somehow as a necessary adjunct of God, an indispensable complement of His being, and therefore eternal as God. This type of thought seems to be so enamored with the idea of God's sovereignty as to overemphasize it, and by its overemphasis on God's lordship it defeats its own end, since God can hardly be said to be the free Lord over a world that is indispensable to His being. The exclusion of both errors hangs together most intimately with the doctrine of creation. In creation as a free and voluntary act of God, He posits the world as the object over which He is sovereign and by that very act establishes His absolute lordship over it.

One may find far more reason for questioning Brunner's agreement with the Biblical doctrine of creation

than for questioning Barth's agreement with it. Nevertheless there is room for asking the question whether
Barth would class God's sovereignty as a relation or as
an attribute. No one can very well mistake the fact
that his emphasis on the lordship of God suggests a
movement away from its conception as a relation toward
its conception as an attribute. We can cordially agree
that God's lordship is deeply rooted in His being; what
is less sure is his agreement to the position that God's
lordship can and should also be viewed as distinct from
His being or essence. The uncertainty in this regard
arises from his peculiar interweaving of the lordship
of God with the trinity of God.

2. *The Sovereignty and the Trinity of God*

We are face to face with one of the numerous points
at which an inquirer into the theological position of
Karl Barth deplores the absence thus far of complete
dogmatics from his pen. All that we have is merely
an introduction to dogmatics: very voluminous, it is
true, but still only an introduction by way of a development of the doctrine of the Word of God. In Barth's
exposition of the doctrine of the Word of God, the ideas
of the Trinity and of the sovereignty of God certainly
occupy much space and play an important role; but it
is all along to be remembered that in his doctrine of
the Word of God, Barth is not saying all that he has
to say about either the Trinity or the sovereignty of God
but only so much as will make clear his conception of
their bearing on the revelation or, as he would say, the
Word of God. For that reason it is hazardous to attempt
on so incomplete a basis a critique of his teachings regarding God's sovereignty and God's Trinity; it is much
safer merely to indicate the connection Barth sees be-

tween the two in their bearing upon the revelation of God.

Let us note, then, that, according to Barth, the Trinity is central and fundamental to the Christian idea of God. He rejects the possibility of first discussing a general idea of the Deity and then subsuming under it the triune God, correctly insisting, that the triune God is the only God Whom we have and can have any knowledge, since He alone is God. He furthermore insists on an essential instead of a merely economic Trinity and underscores the fact that the doctrine of the Trinity bars for the Christian all aberration either in the direction of a pagan plurality of gods of lower and higher rank or in the direction of a monotheism of the Jewish or the Mohammedan type.

Furthermore, it should be noted that according to Barth, the self-revelation of this triune God is objectively real and possible in the incarnation, in Jesus Christ, and that subjectively its reality and possibility lie in the outpouring of the Holy Spirit. In other words, Barth's doctrine of the Word of God draws and leans as heavily upon a Christology and a Pneumatology as it does upon the doctrine of the Trinity. The God that becomes manifest in the revelation is the triune God, and the manifestation of the triune God is the incarnate Son of God, while the primary recipient of the revelation in faith is not the believing sinner but the Holy Spirit as the author of the believer's faith. Barth's Christology and his Pneumatology rest in the approved orthodox fashion upon his doctrine of the Trinity. And if he is asked what the significance of this combination of the doctrines of the Trinity, the incarnation, and the outpouring of the Holy Spirit in the doctrine of the Word of God is, his answer is that thus God reveals

Himself as being the Lord and thrice over subject in
His revelation: viz., as the God Who is revealed, as the
One Who reveals God and as the One Who hears the
revealing Word.

It is difficult to conceive of a close connection between the sovereignty and the trinity of God than is
thus established. Since by common consent the sin of
man consists precisely in his rejection of the sovereignty
of God, no quarrel can be had with a presentation of the
revelation which sees in it an emphasis on God's inalienable lordship. It might not be quite fair to Barth to
suggest that the connection of the Trinity with the lordship of God is not any closer than its connection with
the grace of God, as also His sovereignty and His grace
are most intimately connected. However, one question
remains. We are inclined to think a bit more of a history of the revelation, of progress in the revelation,
than Barth seems in the habit of doing. And it is a
plain fact, that the trinity of God appears on the pages
of the New Testament with far greater clarity than on
those of the Old. But if one fact about God shines
forth luminously from every page of the Old Testament, it is the fact of His sovereignty. In other words,
the history of the revelation gives occasion to question
the particularly close relationship Barth sees between
the trinity and the sovereignty of God. Somehow the
declaration of the sovereignty of God in the midst of a
rebellious world does not seem to have called immediately for an equally clear enunciation of the trinity
of God.

3. *The Sovereignty of God and the Analogy of Being*

Let us proceed to the relationship which God sustains
to the world which He has called into being. To the

medieval Scholastics, the analogy of being was quite essential in this relationship. They argued that since God is the absolute Being and has imparted being to His creatures, something as to the nature of the latter may be inferred from the nature of God and for the nature of God from that of His creatures. We are reminded here of Article II of the Belgic Confession, and we realize that a kernel, at least, of this idea the Reformation carried with it out of the Roman Catholic Church.

It is well known that Barth is emphatically in opposition to the Roman Catholic doctrine of the Analogy of Being and substitutes for it a doctrine of an Analogy of Action, of Doing; viz., God's revelatory act, His speaking, finds its proper analogy in man's hearing, in the believer's faith. It is a question whether such a substitution is at all admissible, whether this analogy of doing does not ultimately rest precisely upon the rejected analogy of being, and whether the elimination of the latter does not fundamentally eliminate all correspondence between God and man from the realm of nature and limit it strictly to the realm of grace.

If Barth's opposition lies against a theology that infers altogether too much from the analogy of being and allows altogether too much influence upon its interpretation of the Bible to such inferences, we can agree. We would not plead for a natural theology that does not at every step subject its positions to the only infallible rule of the Word of God. It should not be imagined, however, that the Medieval philosophers and theologians did not appeal to the Bible for the support of their doctrine of the Analogy of Being in its details as well as in principle. The possibility that they may have been largely mistaken does not at any rate invalidate a natural theology that is drawn from the Bible.

There are a number of other peculiarities in the position of Barth which stand in evident connection with his rejection of the doctrine of the Analogy of Being. He has parted with Emil Brunner, who wishes to operate with an *Anknuepfungspunkt* for saving grace in fallen man, and with Gogarten, who wishes to operate with *Schoepfungsordnungen* as preservatives for human society after the fall of man. When in the debate, Brunner tried to impute what is virtually the Anabaptist position to Barth, I think the latter was successful in showing a difference between what he actually held and what Brunner tried to fasten on him. Yet the impression that Brunner correctly sensed the drift of his former colleague's development is confirmed by the fact that recently Barth has advanced to a denial of the Scriptural basis of infant baptism. In view of this, one feels tempted to reformulate our question thus: Is the Anabaptist conception of the sovereignty of God the same as the Calvinistic conception?

Involved in all these points of dispute is the following question: Have the previous acts of the sovereign God any regulative value for His subsequent acts or have they no such value? The fact that God leaves existence to the reprobate in hell need not be interpreted as an act of kindness toward them, but it may very well be in harmony with the goodness of that God, Who cannot deny Himself; a maintenance of His creative act that brought them into being, just as their torment is a maintenance of His Covenant of Works. Calvinists, who conceive of the creation of which the Bible speaks as a re-creation, certainly hold that God does not repudiate what once He has wrought. Anabaptists, who conceive of the renewal of all things of which the Bible speaks as a new creation, are far closer to the position that God can repudiate what once He has wrought. Where is Barth?

4. *The Relation of Creation and of Sin*

Creation and sin are the two fundamental facts that differentiate man from God. In creation, God imparted to us a being distinct from His own, and in sin we have turned this being of ours against Him. Except for a change in figure, we can have little quarrel with Barth's teaching that the ray of God's revelation reaches us only through a double refraction. In accordance with the principle, that the finite cannot comprehend the Infinite, the creature as such can know God only in a creaturely way and not as God knows Himself. And in the case of sinful man, on top of this comes his rejection and the forfeiture of that pure knowledge of God which would befit him as God's creature and image. Now, the ray of God's revelation to reach us must not merely traverse the infinite distance that lies between the Creator and His creature, but it must in addition penetrate the blindness and darkness that spring from God's wrath and man's corruption.

But for the change in figure, we can agree with Barth. Perhaps Barth's choice of figure is significant. We have our own conception of the relation that obtains between creation and sin. It is not clear that Barth's conception is the same. The infinite distance between the Creator and His creature is there with necessity when once it pleases God to call the finite into being. But the antithesis between the holy God and sinful man is a reality that is not marked with the same necessity. Sin is essentially the repudiation of that relationship to the Lord God which flows with necessity from the fact

that He made us. But sin is not something that flows
with anything like equal necessity from the fact of our
creation. It is not a simple and unavoidable consequence
of creation. We would like to know that Barth agrees
to this. It is not clear that he agrees.

It is true that he lays the responsibility and guilt of
sin and its entrance into man's world solely at the
door of man. On the surface, this would seem to answer
our question whether he agrees in the affirmative. Alas,
other utterances of his make this appearance nugatory!
Speaking with reference to God's special revelation in
Jesus Christ, he holds that God's determination embraces
man's choice. Whether man's choice in response to that
revelation be that of faith or of unbelief, the responsibility for it is solely man's, while yet he chooses either
to believe or to disbelieve just as God in His sovereign
freedom determines. In view of such language regarding the sinner's faith and unbelief the ascription of the
responsibility for man's fall and sin to him alone really
means very little. It can accord perfectly with the hyper-
supralapsarian bald statement that God has willed sin.

Calvinists frankly acknowledge that the precise relation of the entrance of sin into the world to the counsel, or decree, or will of God is beyond our power to
determine, since Scripture does not clear this up. The
universality of sin within the human race, Scripture
connects with the physical and spiritual unity of the
race, but not with the fact that we are creatures, for in
the case of the father of us all it gives us a glimpse
of a state of rectitude prior to his fall. Moreover,
Scripture teaches the entrance of sin into our world
from the world of pure spirits in the sense that they
have nothing comparable to our somatic nature. And in
that angelic world, according to Scripture, sin is not

common to all its members but originated with one and spread only to some of the rest, not to all. We desire from Barth a clear recognition of the fact that according to Holy Writ it is not a corollary of their creatureliness when God's intelligent creatures fall into sin.

5. *Predestination Either an Act or a Decree of God*

Scripture posits our election in Jesus Christ before the foundation of the world. It is in deference to this fact that we are accustomed to group the divine predestination with God's eternal decrees and counsel in distinction from God's works in time by which He executes all that is decreed in His counsel. Barth, however, speaks of the divine election as a deed or act of God rather than as a purpose of God, and he places that deed or act in time rather than in eternity, identifying it with what we would call its execution in the quickening of the sinner to eternal life.

It should be observed that at this point we are face to face with the whole perplexing question of Barth's conception of the relation of time and eternity. His terminology allows him to speak as he does without denying the eternal character of God's election. He conceives of God's eternity and our time as in a sense parallel and running side by side, separated only by the line of death or as being related as the vault of heaven is to this earth, which it overarches. From that overarching eternity, God's act may at any time and place flash down vertically into the horizontal plane of our human life. We can understand and employ that imagery of his, since for us also the difference between time and eternity is qualitative and infinite, and eternity, is not merely an infinite lineal extension backward and forward of our time. But it does not follow that the notions he and we connect with such imagery are, therefore, also the same.

It may be said that as acts of the eternal God, all His acts share in His eternity. But it does not follow that they all share in His eternity in the same fashion or manner. If he so wishes, Barth may say that as an act of God our regeneration shares in His eternity and is, so far, an eternal act; but that does not wipe out the deep difference between the so-called eternity that adheres to our regeneration and the eternity which is proper to the divine election. We would never assent to a cancellation of the foundation of the world or the beginning of time from between God's elective decree and His regenerating grace. The former is placed by Scripture on yonder side of the line, and the latter on this side, and the foundation of the world or the beginning of time from between God's elective decree and His regenerating grace. The former is placed by Scripture on yonder side of the line, and the latter on this, and the foundation of the world or the beginning of time insuperably keep the two apart. In that sense we must maintain that God's election is an eternal act of God and that our regeneration is an act of God in time. The imagery which compares time and eternity with a bounded and an infinite line may be crude and open to abuse and to ridicule, but that does not say that it has not just enough value to illustrate the difference between God's choice and its execution, from a certain angle.

The identification of God's counsel with its execution may be attempted in two ways. The decree may be made to overshadow and submerge the execution, so that the temporal change may vanish before the eternal being. Or the execution may absorb the decree, so that the permanency of the eternal seems to be lost in the instability of time. Barth's type of thought clearly approaches the latter method, and perhaps it is significant that he appears to have difficulty in getting from the incursions into history of God's eternal acts, abiding effects in time.

6. *God's Sovereignty and His Address of the Individual*

Both Barth and Brunner show a marked tendency to emphasize the personal as over against the natural, the fact that man is a person in distinction from the fact that he has a nature. It is fascinating to observe how in their hands this emphasis becomes an impressive means of driving home to man the fact of his responsibility and the unavoidableness of his response, one way or the other, to the Word in which God addresses him, together with the decisiveness of this event. It is in line with and part of this emphasis that Barth conceives of God's sovereignty as exercised through His Word and also that the salvatory function of the Word seems with him quite to obscure and to absorb the order of salvation. One can understand this: such concepts as regeneration, sanctification, and glorification fit into the natural category much better than they fit into the personal category.

It is well, however, to pause and to ask a few questions before taking over this peculiar Barthian personalism. As do most emphases, this Barthian emphasis seems to go hand-in-hand with a suppression of certain other angles of the truth. According to Holy Writ, God's sovereignty is exercised not merely where the message of the Christ comes but also without abatement everywhere in this sinful world beyond the range of the gospel. Moreover, according to Holy Writ, God exercises His sovereignty not merely in the realm of the personal creation, but also in the realms of the subpersonal, in the spheres of both organic and inorganic nature. A due appreciation of these Scriptural facts is necessary for a proper evaluation of the undeniable fact that God also exercises His sovereignty through His Word in personal address of the individual.

Moreover, we have to take cognizance of the fact that according to Holy Writ God's sovereignty in these subpersonal realms is exercised through the same agency that serves it in the personal realm, to wit, the Word of God. By the Word of His mouth were the heavens made, and God spake and the sea brought forth, and the air, and the dry land. And the Word of God, which called into being creatures which are not persons also addresses and alters them after they have come into being. In view of all this, it would be strange indeed if the Word of God could not reach and alter human nature, which comprises more than the personal, in other ways than merely by meeting and addressing them as persons. There may be very good reason why Scripture does not represent all the gracious changes which the sovereign Savior works in His own in terms drawn from the realm of the personal; why, for instance, it speaks of regeneration, which, after the analogy of generations, does not suggest an address of one's person but rather what goes far deeper, a remaking of that person. And again, since glorification also affects man's body, it would seem to involve a quite different operation of the sovereign Word of God than what can be conceived of as falling under the head of personal address.

Speaking of true conversion, the third and fourth of the Canons of Dort expressly distinguish from the external preaching of the gospel and, mark well, from the powerful illumination of the converts' minds by the Holy Spirit, that they may rightly understand and discern the things of the Spirit of God, the efficacy of the same regenerating Spirit that pervades the inmost recesses of the man, opening the closed and softening the hardened heart and infusing new qualities into the will. While I do not wish to suggest that Barth would at all think of repudiating such utterances of the Calvinistic creeds, I doubt seriously that in his presentation they receive their due and proper emphasis.

7. *God's Determination Embracing Man's Choice*

There is a marked difference between what Barth and what Calvin have to say on this subject, the fact notwithstanding that both formally assent to the same thesis. Barth's claim is that in God's address man comes to his choice. Whether that choice is the choice of faith or unbelief, is determined by God, says Barth, while the choice, whatever it is, remains man's responsibility. It should be clearly understood that according to this view, God's determination does not merely embrace and enfold man's possibilities of choice but enfolds and embraces the opposite possibilities and choices equally and in the same way. This is so much the case that Barth views both man's faith and his unbelief as alike arising or originating or generating under the impact of God's personal address of the sinner in His Word, in Jesus Christ.

There are certain Scripture passages that seem to countenance the representation that God's Word and gospel effects faith in the believer and unbelief in the unrepentent equally. Thus Paul says (II Cor. 2: 15-16): "For we are unto God a sweet savor of Christ, in them that are saved, and in them that perish: to the one the savor of death unto death; and to the other the savor of life unto life." Yet it would be obviously out of harmony with Scripture to deduce from such statements that the preaching of the gospel is equally the cause of unbelief and of faith according to God's sovereign good pleasure. For implied in such a conclusion would be the presupposition that prior to the address of the sinner by the sovereign Word of God he is in a sort of neutral state between faith and unbelief. But such a presupposition is not in accord with the fact that prior to the address of God's Word all, whether they come to faith or to rejection of the gospel, are alike sinners, and sin, according to the Bible, is not a mere rather innocuous neutral something but is positively and actively enmity against God, as Barth cordially acknowledges. And it would seem that he cannot escape the necessity of either dropping this acknowledgment from his system or eliminating the view that God's sovereign address generates equally the opposite responses of faith and unbelief.

Without doubt, the preaching of the gospel, if at all taken serious notice of, will, unless saving grace intervenes, elicit, arouse, stimulate, the latent unbelief of the unregenerate heart. But the unbelief is present in the unregenerate heart without and prior to such stimulation. The preaching of the gospel will elicit faith only when accompanied by God's inward effectual calling, when associated with the regenerating grace of God. Without this grace faith cannot be elicited, since it is not there. And this grace of God bestows sovereignly according as He has determined in His counsel before the foundation of the world. We must recognize the fact, therefore, that God's sovereignty is exercised quite differently in the preaching of the Gospel where faith is bestowed than in such preaching of the gospel where faith is not given. This is not saying that in the latter cases there is no room for a varying exercise of God's sovereignty. Not all are hardened in the same degree that Pharaoh illustrates. But the question may very properly be raised whether the address of God's Word in the case of the unbeliever is in any sense so personal, penetrating, and critical as it is in the case of one brought in faith. Certainly for a man to be lost, it is not necessary that he be brought face to face with the Savior with the same clarity and directness which the saved know. If simply nothing happens to a man, he will be lost. And it is in so far definitely wrong to talk loud and long on the decisiveness of God's address as working both faith and unbelief.

Thus it appears that when a Barthian and a Calvinist both say that God's determination embraces man's choice, it is still far from it that they should mean the same thing. The sinner's choice is naturally that of unbelief; it takes sovereign grace to make it that of faith. Barth shifts the necessity of the personal address of God's Word for reaching the decision from Adam to us, his descendants. His relative neglect of God's Covenants in his doctrine of the Word of God is rather surprising, since covenant-making is eminently a matter of the Word. If his dogmatics proper does not correct this, the neglect is bound to set it apart from Reformed dogmatics.

8. *God's Sovereignty and the Believer's Faith*

Very closely connected with the previous point is the Barthian treatment of the assurance of faith; in other words, the relation which in his opinion the faith of the believer sustains to God's sovereignty. Barth claims that we must believe our own faith, that though faith produces certain psychological phenomena, etc., as its indications, yet the indicative value of these phenomena is never unmistakable, and that it is never for us to know, in our case and in any given instance in our own case, whether the response which God's address actually evokes is that of faith or of unbelief, but that this is known only to God in His own sovereign good pleasure. Thus the assurance of salvation is made insecure to the utmost degree, and the great and ultimate disturber of the peace of mind of God's child is seen precisely in the sovereignty of his heavenly Father in Christ Jesus.

In the Psalms, we find many a complaint of God's saints that is born of an experience of God's hiding His face from them, and in the New Testament the exhortations are by no means few that we must strive to enter in at the narrow gate, that we prove ourselves, whether we be in the faith, and that we make our calling and election sure in a godly walk of life. No doubt there is a display of the sovereign freedom of God in the measure of assurance of salvation He metes out to the individual believers, just as there is a display of His sovereign freedom in the fact that He will endow one man with an optimistically inclined temperament and his brother with a predisposition toward pessimism. And it should be recognized that God's dealings with His child in these matters may very well, according to the spiritual needs of that child of God, be ordered with special reference to his realization of his spiritual dependence on God's grace alone and to his realization of the sovereign freedom of that grace of God. But all this is far from seeing in God's dealings with His own such a pure and simple display of His inscrutable sovereignty as Barth suggests.

In the first place, the hiding of God's face is not infrequently due to some evil harbored in the life of the Christian which God is in this way bringing to the attention of His child. And the exhortations to self-examination are due to the fact that we are open to self-deception, which is something entirely distinct from not being at all able to know or learn what our true state before God is. The complaints of God hiding His face are balanced in the Psalms by jubilations in the experience of His favor, and such complaints and jubilations equally show that the believers know and discern that favor of God. God's Word provides us with standards of judgment to be applied to ourselves and, though the judgments we arrive at in their light are relative and not absolute, they do not partake at all of the nature of such fundamental and irremovable, such radical, uncertainty as would follow if only God and not we could know whether our reaction to His Word is that of faith or of unbelief.

After all, it must not be overlooked that the display of God's sovereign freedom in His gracious dealings with His people is not solely and merely an end in itself, but has a definite, positive, gracious purpose, the purpose that they shall grow in grace and in the knowledge of the Lord Jesus. Their recognition of the sovereign freedom of His grace certainly is part and parcel of that purpose, but it is by no means the whole of it. Their recognition of the gracious nature and ends of God's lordly dealings with them is just as much part and parcel of that purpose. To our profession, "Lord, I believe," we may have to add daily, till the day of our death, the humble cry, "Help thou my unbelief";

but the acknowledgment of the unbelief remaining in us is quite distinct from the mistaken claim that God keeps the certainty and truth about our salvation from us; and never can we concede that the great and radical disturber of the peace of God's saints is precisely His sovereignty. For such a concession, we find far too much of grace in the gospel.

9. *God's Sovereignty and Christian Living*

In view of the fact that, according to Barth, the Christian can never be sure of his faith, it is not surprising to find that he can neither be sure of his life and conduct, can never know, outside the moment of God's personal address, whether the life he is leading is Christian, nor what it should be in order to be Christian. According to Barth, God's sovereignty makes Christian ethics radically problematical. He does not mean this in the sense that, as is well known, your actual ethical problems are always likely to run ahead of your solutions, that when your answer is finally shaped, the question has possibly been outmoded. Nor does he have in mind that God's demand is always far more concrete, varying, and searching, than the most loyal application of any system of Christian ethics that men have elaborated can ever hope to meet. Nor does he have reference merely to the fact that far too often men have been pressed into the service of some human ideology dressed in apparently Christian garb. What he means is that God's demand can be known only in the moment of personal address, that that knowledge cannot safely be carried out of the charmed circle or, shall we say, point of that moment, and that consequently the execution of God's demand by us is always made problematical with the identical problematics that remove our faith from our knowledge to God's alone.

It is reported that Barth has recently developed the view that the only thing the church and its members can do for Christ in this world is to suffer for Him. When we remember the long years of service which Barth has given the suffering Church of Nazi Germany, it is not difficult to see how he may have arrived at such a view. It is significant and indicative of his deep antipathy to the Dutch Neocalvinists, that he is reported to have presented that view in the Netherlands, where Reformed believers are trying in their organized Christian activity to *do* something for Christ in a positive way and are, to all appearances, succeeding in doing it in the field of Christian philanthropy and education certainly, if not also, in the field of Christian politics. This activistic attitude of the Dutch Neocalvinists of course also hangs together with the fact that such activities are still possible in the Netherlands. It should not be overlooked that the possibility at this late date of such activity in the Netherlands is in very large part due to the fact that in years gone by a respectable section of the Dutch Church has been willing to suffer for the Christ for their insistence on the need of Christianizing education, social relations, and politics. In their case, their suffering for Christ has borne fruit in the creation of the possibility of Christian action.

Barth may be unwilling to grant this and to accept its implication, that suffering for Christ and positive Christian organized activity are not so mutually exclusive as he is said to claim. Even so, he ought at least to grant that both the Dutch Neocalvinistic activism and his German passivism are historically conditioned, and he ought to avoid the danger, which threatens us all always, of setting up our personal experience as normative by building it up into a system. We cannot very well, in view of all the evidence, think of Barth otherwise than as far bigger than that danger. But if he is, then the explanation of his passivism must be sought in a deeper constitutive principle of his system. And if we look for such, his own finger points to his peculiar conception of the sovereignty of God in its disturbing and unsettling significance for Christian ethics. We prefer to hold to the traditional view, that God's sovereign good pleasure may now call upon His people to suffer for Christ in this world and may then call upon them to be up and doing for Him and will usually provide for them a call to mingled doing and suffering.

10. *God's Sovereignty and Verbal Inspiration*

To us, the stability of the Christian faith and of the Christian life hang together most intimately with the Bible as their only infallible rule and norm, and with its verbal inspiration. To our ears, it sounds strange indeed, when the question is asked: When is the Bible inspired? And yet this impossible question is in all seriousness asked and answered by Barth. And his question is due to the fact that he cannot unequivocally answer that the Bible is verbally inspired always and everywhere because God in His concern for His glory and His commiseration with our needs has once for all made it so.

Taking his stand in the fact that the process of God's revelation in Jesus Christ is not completed, has not reached its goal, unless and until the sinner actually hears the Word of personal address, Barth holds that the Bible is indeed inspired, verbally inspired in the strictest sense, when taken up in the completed circuit of the revelation as it passes from the triune sovereign Lord Who is revealed in it and reaches the Holy Spirit, Who hears the revealing Word in the faith of the sinner. I am not certain whether we should not add that it is verbally inspired also when in personal address the Word of revelation reaches and evokes the unbelief of the unbeliever, nor whether we should not conceive of this result as also a work of the Holy Spirit in man. At any rate, the decisive hearing of the personal address of God is a work of His sovereign and inscrutable free good pleasure, and so is the difference in the response of the believer and the unbeliever. And therefore it follows that the verbal inspiration of the Bible hinges from case to case and from incident to incident and from moment to moment on the inscrutable working of God's sovereign good pleasure in such fashion that the same Bible may in the same hour and moment be inspired in the case of one man and uninspired in the case of the other.

Such a view of the Bible simply refuses to fit into our conception of the totality of reality. There are other points at which the same fundamental difference seems to emerge, such as the church and the individual believer and even the person of Jesus of Nazareth. It is hard to state just wherein the fundamental difference consists. Perhaps it is not too far from the mark to

say that instead of recognizing two sharply distinct
forces as operating in our world, to wit, that of God's
common grace in which all mankind shares and that of
God's special and saving grace, which is strictly limited
to His elect, and allowing to the means of saving grace
a wider sphere of unsaving influence than would embrace the narrow circle of the elect merely, he operates
with the conception of two distinct spheres, to wit, that
of God's eternity and that of man's historicity, and conceives of the sphere of God's eternity as inscrutably in-
truding into the sphere of man's historicity without
becoming at all discernible to any but those upon whom
it momentarily seizes and ceaselessly alternates these
between the two spheres with an abiding uncertainty as to
where they will ultimately land individually.

11. *Barth's Discarded View of Predestination*

This picture that Barth draws of the totality of reality
used to be rather complete as long as he held to the
view of predestination propounded in his *Roemerbrief*.
That view ultimately landed all men in the **sphere of**
God's eternity just as certainly as it provisionally kept
them all in our historicity. Since the claim that Barth
used to be universalistic is being disputed, I shall quote
the passage verbatim in translation. Speaking of the
mystery of eternal double predestination as necessary,
"since only in His election *and* reprobation, love and
hatred, making alive *and* slaying God can become to
this man in this world conceivable and adorable as God,"
he says: "For that very reason, however, it is the mystery of *man, not of this and that man*. It does not
separate between this and that man, but it is their
deepest fellowship. Over against it they all stand in

one line. Over against it Jacob is in every moment of time also Esau, and Esau is in the eternal moment of the revelation also Jacob. Jacob is the imperceivable Esau and Esau the perceivable Jacob. The reformatory formulation of the doctrine of predestination is therefore mythologizing also in this respect, that it has referred election and reprobation to the pyschological unity of the individual, to quantities of 'elect' and 'reprobate.' This is not Paul's meaning, cannot be his meaning. . . ." This might, of course, mean either the ultimate loss or salvation of all, but Barth takes care that we know which of the two is his meaning: "We know what this duality in God signifies: not equilibrium to be sure, but eternal victory over the second by the first: over judgment by grace, over hatred by love, over death by life. But this victory is at every moment of time hid from *us*." I cannot see how anybody can read anything but universalism in these utterances, and the entire context in his commentary on Romans 9 is in perfect harmony.

If Barth were still holding to this view, we might feel forced to supply the unreformed answers to those questions, which we found it necessary to ask without being able to find definite answers in his writings. But this capstone of his system of thought is no longer in place. We are informed that he now concedes that the reformatory formulation of the doctrine of predestination was correct in referring election and reprobation to quantities of individuals. It would be a pleasure, if in consequence we could be certain, that now he no longer robs his emphasis on God's sovereignty and on the decisiveness of the eternal moment of all ultimate value. But for such an assumption, we lack the necessary data.

All that we can say on the basis of our actual observations is that Barth is adrift. He has sailed forth from the modernistic port on a course that took him nearer and nearer to the Calvinistic haven, but as far as appearances go there is greater, far greater probability that he will reach the shores of Anabaptism, to which he is perilously near.

APPLICATORY STUDIES

AND POLITICS

GARRETT HEYNS, PH.D.

THE SUSPICION has entered my mind that my being asked to appear before this august gathering may have some slight connection with the fact that I have had a modicum of experience with an activity of dubious repute, which ordinarily men dub "politics." On occasions I have been introduced as a politician, and that, even when done in jest, has never seemed to me to partake of the nature of a compliment, for I know what is usually in men's minds when they use the term. And so it is with a bit of defense complex that I say at the outset that when, for the purpose of this paper, I use the word "politics," I have no reference to the "skullduggery" and nefarious manipulation that has not infrequently crept into the current method of handling our democracy. I have in mind rather the original sense of the word, that is, the science of government; and when I speak of political activity, I refer to the citizen's participation in the affairs of state.

To the field of political theory, the word "sovereignty" is indigenous. He who reads the literature dealing with other phases of human activity, such as science, art, or industry, may go far without ever encountering the

93

term. This will not be his experience when he interests himself in political science, for here we are concerned with the fact that one man or group of men has authority over others, with the fact that some institution in the nation possesses power over the citizens; and it is to be expected that the thinking man will be desirous of tracing this authority, this power, back to its source. He wants to know who is the ultimate authority, who is really the sovereign. And when the Christian, for whom God is the ruler over all creation, takes up the question of the final source of governmental competence, it is but natural that he should go back to the sovereignty of God.

Thus it was that, after the rise of Christian states, when Medieval thinkers began working on the problem of evolving a political science based upon the principles of Christianity, the dogma of the sovereignty of God was presented — that is, the doctrine that God as the sovereign of the universe is the source of all authority among the nations; that magistrates and kings obtain their power as a mandate from Him. During those days, that truth found general acceptance, and even when the church and state groups waged their conflict as to the supremacy of these institutions, there was no question as to the divine origin of the power of the state; the issue was merely whether the grant of authority to the ruler came directly from God or indirectly through the church.

From the doctrine of the sovereignty of God, the Medieval political scientists derived the authority of the ruler to govern, for he functioned as a mandatee of the Most High. From the same source they established the duty of the subject to obey, for he was to regard the government as the representative of God, to whom he must render obedience. They arrived also at the conclusion that the ordained form of government was that of monarchy and that its function was that of affording protection to the church; for in those days the current view of life was other worldly, and since spiritual matters were the charge of the ecclesiastical body, the secular authority had but to protect it so that it might be the more able to carry out its function. Thus did political relations based upon the dogma of the Medieval thinkers arrive at a statement of the sovereignty of God.

There is no need for presenting here a detailed account of the vicissitudes of the dogma. When once the church of the Middle Ages entered into conflict with the state for supremacy, it lost interest in the tenet, for thereby was threatened the superiority for which the ecclesiastical body was contending. Furthermore, in the course of time, political philosophers arose who sought other bases for the origin and authority of the state than that founded upon the sovereignty of God; they declared that there was sufficient justification of the state in man's social instinct, in the fact that man was a social being. Men began to doubt also that the state must needs have a monarchical form or that its function was merely that of protecting the church. And thus in the field of political thinking, the dogma lost prestige.

A revival of interest in the doctrine was manifest among the theologians and political thinkers of the days of the Reformation. These harked back to the Middle Ages and gave new life to the dogma of the sovereignty of God; they derived from it the principle that both government and governed possessed rights given them by the Ruler of creation. However, a bit later, in the times of the absolutist Stuarts of England and Bourbons of France, the tenet became identified with the theory of the divine right of kings. And when, in the course of time, there arose a reaction against absolutism, theory and doctrine both lost caste.

It is in connection with Calvinism and in countries where Calvin's teachings flourished, that the political implications of the doctrine gained greatest acceptance—this for the reason that Calvinism made the sovereignty of God part and parcel of its world and life view.

So much for the historical setting.

Permit me now to indicate briefly the implications for political relations of this doctrine of the sovereignty of God—not with the purpose of being exhaustive; rather with that of recalling these matters to your attention.

A political science based upon this doctrine holds that one cannot find in man or in any human virtue or dignity the final source of either authority or liberty in the state. Justification for human authority is to be found only in the will of God as He has revealed it.

As to the ruling authority, it implies that government is the servant of God, whom it must recognize as the source of its power. It is God's minister; not His vicar with the possession of unlimited authority. Governmental officials are to obey God and to conduct themselves to His glory. They are to exercise their power in accordance with His ordinances, and to that end they are to investigate what is the will of God. They are to be mindful of the fact that government was instituted to preserve God's creation from the devastating effects of sin. They are to shield good from evil.

For the citizen, the doctrine has the implication that he must obey the government, not from coercion or expediency or because of any claim government may

have on such obedience based upon any virtue of its
own, but because the ruling power in the state derives
its competency from God, Who has ordained that man
shall obey it, and because such command is binding
upon the conscience of the individual. The Christian
citizen obeys consciously and voluntarily because God
so wills. He is a willing coöperator in the affairs of
government, and his participation is prompted by conscience. Certainly a state can wish for no higher
standard of loyalty and obedience than this.

However, there is an implication of another duty for
the citizen besides that of obedience to the governmental
authority. Government was instituted to bring about
order and discipline in a world which, but for that institution, would have reverted to chaos. It does not
exist for the glorification of man or to lend itself to
the creation of a despotism that recognizes no power
outside of itself nor gives consideration to any man
or institution. It follows, therefore, that tyranny, or
abuse of power, on the part of rulers is not to be toler-
ated. This means that there rests upon the people an
obligation to protect their liberties, and from this fact
follows the duty of intelligent participation on the part
of the citizen in political affairs. Let me emphasize
that taking part in elections, holding office, noting government policies, keeping a watchful eye on the conduct
of officials, and protesting against abuses when need
arises, guarding against the perils that may threaten
our personal liberties in the power of the state, and
being the sort of understanding and informed citizen
upon whom the state can absolutely rely is not a matter
of choice or convenience. For a Calvinist, it is a duty
to which he is bound by the will of God, by his confession of the sovereignty of God. And should there

occur a conflict between liberty and authority, a conflict in which the government appears to be drifting toward a despotism, there arises the duty of the citizen to seek redress through such legal means as are available. Thus cases may arise when refusing to obey becomes a right and a duty. This love of liberty, which is the ordained means for preventing the state from degenerating into despotism, is a possession the Christian must guard.

Government is not unlimited in its authority. It is limited impliedly by the purpose for which it was instituted, by its duty to heed the ordinances of God as He has revealed them and by the rights appropriate to the people. It is limited farther by the fact that there are special institutions in society such as the family, the church, art, science, commerce, and industry—which owe neither their origin nor the law of their life to the state, but to God Himself, even as does the state. To these God has given special tasks and also the right to perform their special functions to His glory. These rights are to be respected by the state, and interference therewith cannot be condoned. Furthermore, government must have regard for the individual conscience, for the respect to conscience every man is sovereign with no power above him save the Almighty.

Incidentally, this matter of the sovereignty of certain spheres is of interest in connection with much of the social, industrial, and economic legislation and regulation being enacted these days both in our own country and abroad. It raises the question: to what extent is this type of legislation permissible? When does it represent an invasion on the part of the government into the peculiar right of these spheres? Naturally it is an outright and intolerable invasion when such legislation interferes with the ability of these institutions to per-

form their special functions. To the extent that it is enacted in the interest of the common good and is aimed
at preventing such spheres from hindering the common
welfare, such legislation is permissible. Here we must
weigh measures calmly and dispassionately. A Calvinist
cannot tolerate state omnipotence such as is evident in
present-day manifestations of Communism and Fascism.
Nor can he permit a special institution such as industry
and commerce, under the claim of autonomy, to seek
justification for conditions and acts that may interfere
with the common well-being. I have previously said
that in the Middle Ages political theories deduced from
the doctrine of the sovereignty of God the conclusion
that the indicated form of government was that of
monarchy. One would be inclined to expect such conclusion since they must needs express themselves in
those forms with which they had had experience. The
fact is that the authority of government comes from
God alone; however, the form through which that authority is exercised is not pertinent save only that it
be recognized that the power of the rulers is limited in
the ways we have indicated. The form a government
should assume is a matter of expediency rather than
of divine prescription. One form fits one nation; another works more effectively among other peoples. It
does not matter, save only with the limitations noted.
It would, I suppose, be a truism to say that that form
is best that most effectively meets the purpose for which
government was instituted.

   To sum up this section of the paper, let me quote:
"So the political significance of the doctrine of the
sovereignty of God for political relations implies that
it forbids the degrading of government as a mandatee
of sovereign man, as well as the debasement of man to

a rightless object of an arbitrary and omnipotent state, and that it claims the coöperation of government and people, each according to his own duties, which God, the Sovereign of both, granted to each of them to the glorification of His name" (Anem). "It is therefore a political faith which may be summarily expressed in these three theses: 1. God alone is possessed of sovereign rights, in the destiny of nations, because God alone created them, maintains them by His power, and rules them through His ordinances. 2. Sin has in the realm of politics, broken down the direct government of God, and therefore the exercise of authority, for the purpose of government, has subsequently been vested in man, as a mechanical remedy. 3. In whatever form this authority may reveal itself, man never possesses power over his fellow-men in any other way than by an authority which descends upon him from the majesty of God" (Kuyper).

Granted that all I have thus far said to be true, where do we go from here? For from the very nature of the case, a consideration of the sovereignty of God and political relations cannot remain in the realm of mental gymnastics; there must follow some practical considerations. Thus the question arises: just how does the confessor of the sovereignty of God play a practical part in the business of government?

Let us remember, to begin with, that there is no room for otherworldliness in all of this. You cannot say: politics in our country is a messy business; best that we withdraw from it; best that the Christian keep out of it lest some of its messiness cleave to him. That attitude just simply will not do. If, as we confess, the authority of the government to rule is derived from God and must be exercised according to His will, who is

there to see to it that this is done but God's own people?
And if, and that is our own belief, too, the people have
certain fundamental rights, also given them by God,
which they must maintain, not because such liberties
are pleasant but from a sense of duty, who is there
to do this—who alone will do it with a feeling of high
obligation but God's own people? And again, if the
sovereignty of God over all creation demands that His
will be carried out with respect to all things, who is
there to strive to that end but the very confessors of
that doctrine? No, rather than asserting that we should
eschew participation in political affairs lest we compromise our Christianity, let us say that the reverse is
true—you cannot neglect politics and remain a Calvinist.
For to us the center of Christianity is not the felicity
of man but the glory of God. Therefore, the test of an
individual's religion is his effort to glorify God in
action. A Calvinist disagrees with the thought that one
must passively endure the world; he feels that he must
be interested in all phases of human activity, must work
within the world itself with the purpose of making all
of life accord with the will of God. And so he must
interest himself in politics as well—not primarily to
further the interests of the body politic, but to glorify
God.

Among us, the opinion is current that politics is a
sordid business. And it often is—how sordid it really
is many of us do not even suspect. Why is that true?
There is surely nothing inherently base in administering
the affairs of our democracy, in pursuing the God-given
right and duty of participating in the affairs of government. The contrary is true, and it is really appalling
to observe that managing machinery of an institution
which derives its authority from the sovereignty of God

should often have so evil a reputation. Why has this state of affairs come to pass? The answer is that we—we Christians—have permitted it. We have avoided political activity and have in many instances left it to those whose ideals of statecraft were close to the earth, and now our politics frequently reflects the ethics of those who manage them. There lies the reason for graft, political manipulation for selfish ends, bribery, and the like. None the less, what we can do when we become sufficiently interested or incensed is apparent from sporadic purifications of local politics throughout the country. Unfortunately, those who delight in using government in city and state merely sit back and wait for the reform movement to lose strength, for well they know that we shall soon turn our attention to what we consider our own affairs under the pleasing delusion that one victory wins a war—incidents Lincoln Steffins describes so often in his *Autobiography*. The political manipulator knows far better than we do that eternal vigilance is the price one must pay for political control. We Christians should bend every effort to see to it that the government functions well because of an appreciation of our duty to God and from a sense of gratitude for His gift, while the so-called "politician" is motivated only by selfishness—yet, and the commentary is a sad one, the latter motive so often seems to be the stronger. Such things ought not so to be. It is time that we awoke.

What practical program are we to follow so that we can the more effectively make our influence felt? It should seem evident, to begin with, that we Calvinists cannot *belong* to our present political parties. I do not mean that we may not on occasion participate in their councils or vote for their nominees. I mean, rather,

that we may not in season and out of it regard ourselves as members of one of these parties, the party as
ours. This holds for the reason that these parties are
not based upon any of the principles such as those upon
which the Calvinist would base his political science.
Oh, it is true, that one citizen may endeavor to prove
that his party is the advocate of fundamental human
rights; and another may try to demonstrate that his
is the bulwark of decency and property rights. All of
that is but a passing phase. They are parties of expediency with platforms based upon the exegencies of
the moment. As the demands vary, so do the platforms,
and presently one group stands where the other stood
in former years. Furthermore, these platforms are not
of our making; we never, as a group, have any hand
in their formulation. And we have no right blindly to
adhere to them when we have no means of knowing what
the planks or policies will be, for these organizations
have no fundamental principles that govern practical
considerations.

We might consider the idea of forming an independent
political party of our own—a Calvinistic political organization. The success of our brethren in the land of
the dykes in their venture into this field might move us
to try the plan. It would seem a grand idea, but perhaps we should be wise and recognize time and circum-
stance. By all means, have our people meet together
to study fundamental political principles, to familiarize
themselves with our views. But we are too small a
group in this expansive land of ours to do anything
effectively as an independent political party. We need
the support of other groups if we are to accomplish
anything, and an organization with a set of principles
like those drawn up for the "Anti-Revolutionaire

Partij," however grand they may be, would scare off others who might otherwise interest themselves in our objectives.

None the less, the way toward effective action under the circumstances lies along the line of independent organization—not as a separate party, with platform, policies, and candidates of its own, but as a mobile political unit, ready to throw its support wherever approved plans are projected or satisfactory nominees are brought forward, prepared also to assume leadership in drives to remedy unsatisfactory conditions in the body politic.

Anyone with some acquaintance with present-day partisan politics knows that in high political council comparatively little attention is given the groups— ethnic, geographical, industrial, and others — whose party loyalty is unquestioned. But upon those whose vote from year to year is unpredictable and whose support is given only as a *quid pro quo*, considerable thought is spent. Party chiefs make concessions to such groups, for they want the support of any small margin that may mean the difference between victory and defeat. Furthermore, whenever their intentions are not as honorable as they should be, they dread the opposition of any group that will fearlessly inform the public of any contemplated "skullduggery."

My thought is that in every community where such can be effected, we bring together representatives of the various local church groups. There should be associated with these representatives, in each of the groups, a number of men who will form a nucleus of workers whenever activity is called for. I don't think there is need for organization beyond that point, at least not wholly. These representatives will make a study of politic affairs, of policies and issues, of candidates for office, and disseminate such information to their constituents. There should be no connection with any political party. The organization should work for the election of such nominees as are acceptable and for the defeat of those who are not; it should be watchful of the manner in which public officials fill their positions of trust, of public morals, and of the manner in which laws and ordinances are enforced, ready to lead a campaign to correct whatever unsatisfactory conditions become apparent. At the outset, interest should center in local affairs, and without doubt much can be done there in effective manner. It is possible that the scope of activity can later be broadened, even to the extent of the formation of an independent party.

Such organization, to be worth while, must be permanent. It is not difficult to arouse public interest in an occasional local issue. However, if we are going to work to make the will of God shape our political relations, we must be active all the time. Sporadic activity is of little avail. Those who have not our ideals will merely wait until our interest has died, and that is something we who are to work for the glorification of God in action cannot allow.

Now, someone may say: "There you go. Wipe out the lines of distinction. Present a sort of attenuated Calvinism. Refuse to hew to the line for fear of scaring off others. That is the sort of pusillanimity that weakens our forces." I don't think that I may, in what I have written, be justly accused of such charge. I have advocated organization for political action on a broad basis, because our numbers are too small to do anything effectively in any other way. Let those others who aid us have such motives as they may—common decency in

politics, for instance—ours is to shape the things of
government according to the will of God. And I would
have our leaders continue to inform our people on the
nature of a political science based upon the doctrine
of the sovereignty of God. However, is it not pertinent
to ask, just what sort of lines have we Calvinists of late
been drawing in this country in the field of political
action? Here we have been altogether without color.
A bit of noble political doctrine we have had, it is true,
but that is all.

The thought that our government's authority and our
rights as citizens are linked directly to the sovereignty
of God is a grand doctrine. The belief that God is
sovereign of the universe and would have His will carried out throughout all fields of human activity—
politics as well—is a solemn one. The reminder that
God wants His followers to do their work toward making
His will manifest in human relations is an arresting
one. I am merely asking you to do your bit toward it.

AND PHILOSOPHY

THE REV. DR. L. DE MOOR

IT was my privilege, in the summer of 1935, while engaged in study at the University of Chicago, to hear Professor T. V. Smith of the Philosophy Department of the University give a popular lecture on what he called "The Philosophic Way of Life." He presented what he considered to be the three fundamental ways in which men "use their heads" in formulating a creed for life and discussed them in what appeared to him their ascending order of importance.

First, then, and least important, is *The Religious Way of Life*: This way of using our heads, he said, will always be most congenial to that group of people whose make-up is such as to constrain them to look up to some supernatural power to give them solace and peace. They are the "tender-minded folk" of Wm. James's classification, in contrast with "the tough-minded." They look about them and discover a world full of evils—cosmic and social. They cannot tolerate the idea that this ought to be thus, and so they imagine that there exists a Being somewhere who is good, perfectly good. This in part soothes them. But presently they are forced to recognize that their thinking thus does not change things. Evils continue. And so in time we find that they add the attribute "power" to this imagined God. This power, added to the Deity, enables man to envision Him as destroying evil, if not at once, then at least eventually; so that in the end the good will triumph. This is the general way in which religious conceptions have come into existence, according to the professor.

In his estimation, this is the weakest and the least important philosophic way of life. He told us that he had personally rejected this way of "using his head." And he gave this as his fundamental reason: The continued presence of evil in the world. If religion is right, this ought not to be the case. But because it is so, there is a double contradiction in the religious way of life. For if God exists, and as such could do away with evil but refuses to do so, then He is not good: on the other hand, if He has the desire or wish to do away with evil but cannot do so, then He is not all-powerful. God is, therefore, neither all-good nor all-powerful. And since it is these very attributes that constitute the being of God if He exists, He is thereby proved not to exist. The unchecked continuance of evil in the world presents us with an insoluble dilemma, which constrains one to the position of Atheism. Of course, a religious person, not to say a Calvinist, instinctively refuses to accept this conclusion and realizes at once that there is something radically wrong with this reasoning; though what the error is may not be so immediately apparent. We shall return to this later, for our first concern is to follow the progressive logic of Professor Smith.

He went on to say that when one has come to "see through" religion there next presents itself *The Scientific Way of Life.* This is a better way of "using our heads" than the use to which the religionist puts it, for whereas the religionist looks up for what he fails to find here on earth, the scientist stays closer to the facts, although he, too, looks beyond them—he directs his vision downward. The scientific approach is "genetic"—it looks to "origins," "backgrounds," "sources." The scientist lives on problems, every one of which he proposes to solve by tracing things back to primordial beginnings. He is just as dissatisfied with the present as is the religionist. The only difference is that whereas the latter looks up for his solution, the scientist looks down for an answer to the riddle of the universe.

Yet, the scientist, too, fails to find the solution of his problem: fails just as miserably as the religionist. For science is today, and always has been—and always will be—"in flux," in a condition of incessant change. Science has never yet settled anything by probing into the origin of things. Witness the contradictory theories of contemporary scientists in every field of knowledge! The essence of science is theory and hypothesis. But who can live by such uncertain speculation? Who can continue to live on the "dry dust" of conjectures? No, science, too, has been weighed in the balance and found wanting; it, too, does not get rid of the cosmic and social evils; it merely discloses a new array of them. The downward look is just as unsatisfactory as the upward look.

Since, therefore, the scientific approach, too, has been weighed in the balance and found wanting, there remains but one more way of "using our heads," in the opinion of Professor Smith, but that, however, is the highest wisdom of life: *The Aesthetic Way of Life.* If the upward look brings us no satisfaction because it leaves us in the midst of unmitigated evils; and if the downward look proves to be equally misleading because it gives us no firm footing, it is because they both share the common error: they both look away from the present. Why not cease looking up and why not cease digging down into the hidden causes of things? Why not rather enjoy the present? Why not live on the horizontal plane of life? This is the proposal contained in the Aesthetic way of life.

This will liberate us completely. It will free our minds from the necessity of asking the futile question: Why are not things different from what they are? It will at once dispose of that otherwise troublesome question of evil. We shall be free to enjoy what is to be enjoyed and honestly ignore the senseless questions about any further meaning of things than their present appearance. We shall be free from the useless supernatural, free from the endless annoying experiments of the scientist to explain our present world. We shall be free from the idle speculations of the experimentalists who are forever in search of the magic key, or the magic stone whereby everything may be turned to gold. Why not rather relentlessly face the facts and admit with candor that both the way of religion and of science leave our problems "in solution"? Why not live on the horizontal plane of life and "eat, drink, and be merry, for tomorrow we die"? We see, then, that it was an unabashed hedonism the learned professor recommended as the deepest wisdom of life. This is his personal creed, his prescription on the "best way of using our heads."

It is obvious that as Christians we are obliged, as over against such an audacious presentation, to work out, and as confidently to present to the world the

Christian philosophy of life, or as Peter puts it, as
Christians "be ready always to give an answer to every
man that asketh [us] a reason of the hope that is in
[us]," even if it is "with meekness and fear" that
we are commanded to do such.

First, then, we must ask: What is Professor Smith's
false assumption in the conception of God, in its bearing
upon the problem of evil? The same evening of the lecture it was my privilege to discuss this address with a
Zoroastrian student of the University as we sat at the
table in the dining-room of the Chicago Theological
Seminary. She had been present at the lecture, and I
asked her judgment. She replied that she believed his
error lay in ascribing the existence of evil and its
continuance in the world to the wrong source. He had
referred this, she said to Ahura Mazda (God of Light,
her name for the Deity), rather than to Ahriman (Prince
of the Kingdom of Darkness, her name for Satan, the
devil). And though the Christian does not agree with
the Zoroastrian in ascribing all evil to an evil principle
which existed from eternity and always ran parallel
with the eternal good, for this would be "cosmic dual-
ism"—but rather believes that evil had a temporal
beginning — yet the Christian analysis of Professor
Smith's error does not differ essentially from that given
by this Zoroastrian.

Holding God responsible for the evil in the world is
much like holding the ingenious Dutchman Koster, (or
whoever it was that invented movable type), responsible
for all the harm that has subsequently been done to mankind through the abuse of the printed page. Instead of
giving God the blame for the existence and continuance
of evil in the world, as does Professor Smith, we ought
to adore a God who is so good that He made man a free

moral agent rather than a blind automaton. For I make
bold to say that a free moral agent, capable of real
choice, even though one of these alternatives could be
the choice of wrong, is higher in the scale of eternal
values than a blind automaton which, without deliberate
intention, undeviatingly keeps a straight course. This
does not excuse sin by explaining it nor shift the responsibility of man's wrong choice upon God. Instead
of that, it vindicates God in His creation of man and
should cause us to have a proper appreciation of the
true glory of man—free moral agency.

Professor Smith boasts that if he had had his way in
the making of the world, he would not have allowed
for even the possibility of evil. Thus he raises himself
up as a critic of God. His, therefore, is a religion of
self-admiration; it is a substitute—and what a poor substitute—for what will always be the essence of all true
religion—adoration—even when we cannot resolve such
problems as that of evil—nay, just because we cannot
do so.

But what shall we say of Professor Smith's criticism
of the genetic approach of the sciences? I incline to
agree with him regarding the hopelessness of the so-
called scientific method, if he is right in saying that
the sole object of science is merely to seek to recon-
struct the so-called purely natural and physical links
in an endless chain of regression, a chain which really
ends nowhere. If that is what the scientific quest is,
we might as well confess that we are on a wild-goose
chase; for it will never be possible to trace the progressive stages whereby mud, by intrinsic forces residing
in it, has, even in a million years been able to produce
the faintest glimmering of a thought or the spark of a
moral ideal.

But if you define science as the exploration of the universe and the story of man's attempt to carry out the Creator's original command, "to have dominion and to subdue," and thus to "think God's thoughts after Him"—to see the divine purposes and plan unfold in the very fabric and process of nature, then the scientific way of life is in no way contradictory to the Christian or Calvinistic religious way of life. They are not only reconcilable but the deepest religious life implies the necessity of some appreciation of God's thought as contained in the glories of physical nature with which we are surrounded and in which our natural life is daily bathed. It was the entertainment of a thoroughly Christian philosophy that enabled Johann Kepler, awed by the marvels of the starry heavens, to burst out in exultation: "O God! I thank Thee that I can think Thy thoughts after Thee!" The Christian philosophy of life is not summed up in the word "exploitation"—not a thoughtless, blind, selfish, or even disinterested examination of nature; but it is best expressed in the word "exploration"—not a disclosing only of the secondary causes but a discovery of the original primary cause, the matchless thought of an all-wise God.

Similarly, the Christian way of life does not exclude the values of Aesthetics. The great Christian apologist, Justin Martyr, said: "Whatsoever things have been rightly said by all men, is the property of us Christians." Because as Calvinists we believe in the doctrine of Common Grace, we should have no difficulty in agreeing with Justin Martyr. In fact, we believe we may interpret this saying to mean, among other things: "Whatsoever things have ministered to the genuine enjoyment of all men everywhere, is the property of us Christians." Paul, exhorting his readers against an unnatural asceticism and world-flight, said with special emphasis: "Rejoice, and again I say, rejoice." And on another occasion he said: "God hath given us all things richly to enjoy." And the Psalmist is no kill-joy, for he is convinced that "at His right hand are pleasures forevermore."

Nevertheless there is a radical difference between the Christian aesthetic view of life and that advocated by Professor Smith. Because the Christian cannot possibly have a satisfaction in living on the horizontal plane, there are no true pleasures for him on this plane. For the Christian, all present, as well as all lasting joys, derive their meaning and content from a consciousness of their derivation from a divine source, in which they are sanctified. The Christian's enjoyments are all bathed in the atmosphere of appreciation. But because in Professor Smith's aesthetics that upward look is lacking, his aesthetics have degenerated to the level of mere selfish appropriation—pure, unadulterated hedonism.

The burden of our thought is this: That the Christian philosophy of life is not narrow but exceedingly broad. Ours, as Calvinistic Christians, is a full-orbed, a completely rounded life. We are far from provincial; in fact we are the only truly cosmopolitan folk on God's earth: "All are yours, and ye are Christ's; and Christ is God's" (I Cor. 3: 22-23). Christianity, especially as interpreted in the Calvinistic tradition, does not present us with a choice between religion, science, and aesthetics. It does not say, "Either choose this or that"; but it says, "Incorporate into your life both this and that, for all have their source and ultimate meaning in God." The Christian way of life makes a challenge to the whole personality. It does not advocate a religion of self-admiration but rather of adoration. It does not

foster a science of exploitation but rather one of exploration. It does not entertain an aesthetics of appropriation
but rather of appreciation. It says with Alfred Lord
Tennyson, the great theological poet of the nineteenth
century:

> *Let knowledge grow from more to more,*
> *But more of reverence in us dwell;*
> *That mind and soul, according well,*
> *May make one music as before,*
> > *But vaster.*

"Vaster"—yes, that is it; because God Himself is the
inexhaustible fountain from which wells up everything
man is or can ever hope to be. But enough in pursuance
of the line of thought suggested by Professor T. V.
Smith.

However, this same error of which the philosopher
is guilty, the error of the false antithesis, also manifested itself in the thinking of many religious philosophers in the last years. We, therefore, next invite you
to consider with us, how, in connection with a wide-
spread view of revelation entertained during the last
two centuries, we have another illustration of this error
of putting asunder what God has meant to be joined
together.

I think that you will agree with me that there are few
more insistent problems in the religious thought of our
day than that of revelation. Especially the growing
spirit of secularism has been and is everywhere threatening the distinctively religious or spiritual conception
of things. Christianity has not escaped this pervasive
influence. As a consequence, the idea of revelation,
when not completely abandoned, as it has been by some,
has more often been subjected to important modifica-
tion. It is characteristic of important currents of thought

in the last two hundred years that the concept of the transcendent is considered superfluous in any field of thought. John Dewey's theological views, as expressed in *A Common Faith,* are a logical culmination of this stream of thought. According to this point of view, revelation should be considered as issuing from those natural human attitudes which realize themselves in a pursuit of "ideal ends." Moreover, the God-idea, it is argued, should be surrendered or should only be thought of as symbolizing human ideals and hopes. It is claimed that the human "imagination" presents these ideals to man and his will quite naturally responds to them as worthy of pursuit. That which results, we are told, may be called revelation. All this not only happens in the course of man's natural life but there is no need for or justification of referring anything in this experience to a transcendent realm. This new piety, rather than placing a premium upon an acknowledgment of ignorance, centers its loyalty upon the relentless employment of the method of scientific inquiry. Salvation is reached only by some kind of self-discipline: it is a natural and immanent process. Thus at every point it is claimed that if we are to retain the concept or revelation it must be rethought in terms of immanent laws and conditions. Professor Pauck does not state the issue too strongly when he says: "Whether there can be a religion without God, a godless religion, is the question which constitutes the present crisis of religion" (William Pauck—*Karl Barth, Prophet of a New Christianity?*—p. 11).

Thus the problem before us today is: The validity of the concept of revelation itself. We are challenged to reconsider whether or not the following pairs are mutually exclusive: the natural and the supernatural,

the objective and the subjective, the rational and
the suprarational, the autonomous and the divinely
prompted, the scientific and the authoritative, the ethical
and the historical. Even certain so-called "naturalistic"
or "humanistic" thinkers profess not to deny the reality
of revelation nor to reject the belief that the content
of revelation is divine. They insist, however, that this
divine content will never supersede or transcend natural
conditions. The traditional view, on the other hand,
has been that there is and can be no valid concept of
the "divine" apart from a transcendent supernatural
reference.

Adherents of the traditional view who emphasize the
transcendent nature of the revelation content do not
deny that revelation is transmitted to man over path-
ways that are a part of external or internal nature. But
the persistent question that remains is whether, in the
last two centuries of religious thought, the divine content of revelation has been kept inviolate while at the
same time the human media have been recognized as
the indispensable channels of its transmission. The
problem of revelation is to correlate the supernatural
content with the historical processes by means of which
it has been revealed and to do justice at once to the
superhuman fact and content and the human media and
conditions of the revelation.

The problem of necessity revolves around these two
focuses, for it is involved in the very conception of
revelation that the human spirit is intimately related
to the divine and that there is an interaction between
them. Because revelation, the disclosure of the divine,
is always realized through some human medium, it has
proved to be an ever recurring temptation for theologians in the last two centuries to disengage and divorce

the divine elements from the human. But it was in
yielding to this temptation that the error of abstraction
has too often been made, either to the disadvantage of
the divine, or transcendent element, or to the neglect
of the human channels. The obligation to disentangle
the divine and human elements too frequently has been
taken so seriously that the necessity of maintaining an
organic union of the factors has been neglected.

In an important sense, and speaking broadly, this
struggle has been one between faith and reason, the
Barthians championing the former and the Lessing-
Schleiermacher-Ritschlian tradition representing the latter. The slogan of the first group may be said to be the
classical utterance of Tertullian: *Credo, quia absurdum
est* ("I believe because it is absurd") and that of the
other group the modern-sounding, but none the less
classical formula of Abelard: *Credo, ut intelligam* ("I
believe in order that I may understand"). Now, if
there is anything the history of Christian doctrine in
our modern period should have taught us, it is this:
that it is invalid to set these two conceptions over
against each other as mutually exclusive. This is not
a case of "either-or" but of "both-and." It is a false
and unwarranted antithesis to cut the two ideas asunder.
It is true, and a conception for the emphasizing of which
the Barthians, in our day, should be given due credit
and honor, that faith involves the irrational, the in-
comprehensible, the paradoxical, the wholly Other.
Without this there could be no talk of revelation at all,
for without it there would be nothing to reveal. But it
defeats the very possibility of revelation to insist, as they
do, that there is no point of contact (*Anknüpfungspunkt*)
whatsoever between the divine and the human, no con-

tinuity whatsoever, even though it be the divine initiative itself that throws the connecting bridge.

Rather, revelation is an organic union of the divine and the human. If there were no community between God and man, He could not reveal Himself. Even if He spoke, we should be unable to hear Him; we should lack the faculty even of conceiving His existence. Not only so, but any revelation He might make would have no meaning for us. It follows, then, that if God reveals Himself to man, there must be something in man that can respond to Him. As Pascal has so beautifully put it, "Thou couldst not seek Him had'st Thou not already found Him." Revelation comes from without, as a great light, yet it manifests what has always been present to us. "In Thy light we shall see light" (Ps. 36:9). There is an inner light of the "Logos," "which lighteth every man that cometh into the world," of which the incarnate, the visible, the tangible, the historical Logos Who was "made flesh" (John 1:14) serves as the complement. As a creature of the natural order, man is endowed with senses and faculties that make him capable of answering its requirements; but there is that in him which allies him to another and higher order. In the act of creating him as man, God placed His own mark upon him and gave him a knowledge of Himself which no abuse has ever been able to eradicate completely. These human conditions of receptivity constitute the subjective elements of revelation and are as truly parts of the organic conception as the content that exists objectively.

Therefore, in the language of the Post-Kantian idealistic theology, it may truly be said that "all knowledge rests upon experience"—also knowledge of the divine; so that revelation, too, must of necessity come by the road of experience. It is true, as Luther himself said: *Deus non abit donis suis* ("God is not absent from His gift"); God, the objective cause, is not to be conceived as foreign to or absent from the experienced gift of revelation. Yet it is not adequate to look to God, as has too frequently been done in the last two centuries, as the transcendent "reference" to which human experience merely points—the "Source," the "Whence," to Whom we can reason back in a causal series or to which we are intuitively led back under the compulsion of inner experience (Schleiermacher). This either makes God artificially external to the inner experience or grants to experience itself the prerogative of disposing of the divine, of wielding lordship over Him who is Himself arbiter of our destinies. We need a conception of revelation which, while safeguarding the unique glory of man, the recipient of revelation, does not ride roughshod over the divine prerogative and supernatural content.

Just such a union of the objective and subjective as we have discovered the need of has unquestionably from the beginning underlaid Christian thought concerning revelation, at least whenever the Scriptures of the Old and New Testaments were permitted to serve as the criterion or norm. For

"In the Old and New Testaments alike, both conceptions find their place. God is the high and holy one, reigning in heaven, and yet there is always the sense of man's affinity with God. Man is made in God's image and receives from Him the breath of life. God dwells with the humble and contrite heart; He has made us for Himself; He has searched and known us, and we are continually with Him" (E. F. Scott, *The New Testament Idea of Revelation*, p. 11).

It is necessary merely to call attention to the Biblical doctrines of creation, preservation, incarnation, and resurrection, in each of which the organic union of the divine and the human is emphatically expressed.

Though it may be the accident of birth and ecclesiastical connection that predisposes the writer in the formation of his personal conclusions on this subject, it has seemed to him nothing less than remarkable that in what for convenience we may call the Augustinian-Calvinistic-Reformed tradition a remarkable balance and symmetry has been maintained respecting these two factors.

The framework of Augustine's philosophy of the Christian religion, which is also his doctrine of revelation, is this: Matching the divine essence, which approaches us from without, is the inner human self-consciousness, man's subjective capacity, which in response to the Deity assimilates a certain valid knowledge of the same, though in this earthly life never a complete knowledge. On this point Wilhelm Windelband aptly sums up St. Augustine's teaching:

For His incorporeal and changeless essence (*essentia*) far transcends all forms of relation and association that belong to human thought" (Wilhelm Windelband, *A History of Philosophy*—Tr. by James H. Tufts, 2d ed.—revised 1926—p. 276).

Nevertheless, the two together constitute an organic whole and without both the revelation is not possible, in Augustine's view.

The following is a summary of Calvin's theory of knowledge, classified in terms of the two elements that constitute the knowledge relationship in respect to things divine:

The subjective side of revelation consists of:
1. The ineradicable human capacity to know and worship the Creator in spite of the universal abuse thereof.
2. The implantation of faith, i.e., the constraining inward

operation of the Holy Spirit, whereby the objectively wrought manifestation of Deity is made internally effective in human lives.

The objective side of revelation consists of:
1. The divine glory as reflected in
   a) The mirror of external physical nature, and
   b) The human constitution (physical and psychical).
2. The Scriptures of the Old and New Testaments, which serve both
   a) as the key for the understanding of the otherwise unlocked mysteries of the glories of nature, and
   b) for the exposition of the doctrine of salvation, centered in the life and work of Christ.

The historical manifestation of God Himself in the incarnate Christ.

It is fallacious to reserve the term revelation only for the objective factors and then either to call the original subjective element "natural religion" or to deny that the latter factor has any bearing upon religion or revelation at all. The inward, antecedent, or prior revelation, implicit in our very being, affords the point of contact between God and man. Without a common language there can be no instruction, and before God can speak His message, we must have the capacity for understanding Him.

Yet from the inward revelation alone, man could never know God. Those instincts in him which reach out to something beyond would lie dormant and could excite nothing more than a bewilderment and vague discomfort. The inward premonition begins to have meaning only when it meets with an answer. A message must come to it from without which makes it conscious of itself, as sounds come to a child and acquaint him with his sense of hearing. It is a fact of experience that the consciousness of God has always to be quickened by an impulse from without. These two aspects, which

even a sound psychology would seem to demand, are
not only preserved in the Calvinistic conception of
revelation, but are here formed into an organic whole,
a synthetic unity.

Also, Dr. Herman Bavinck has so beautifully expressed the hand-and-glove relationship between the objective and subjective factors that we have discovered
constitute the present problem of revelation, that we
give the passage in full:

> "Consequently, to the objective revelation of God, there
> corresponds in man a certain faculty or aptitude of his nature
> to recognize the divine. God does not leave His work half
> finished. He not only creates the light, but also the eye to be-
> hold that light. The external corresponds to the internal. The
> ear has been fashioned for the world of sounds. The 'logos'
> in the items of created nature corresponds to the 'logos' in
> man and make science possible. Beauty in nature finds an
> answering echo in aesthetic sensibility. Likewise there is not
> only an external, objective revelation, but an internal, sub-
> jective revelation as well. The former is the *principium cog-
> noscendi externum* of religion; the latter is the *principium
> cognoscendi internum*. Both 'principia' stand related to each
> other in the most intimate fashion, like the light to the eye, and
> like rationality in the world to the human reason" (Herman
> Bavinck, *Gereformeerde Dogmatiek*, vol. I, p. 253. Translation
> is my own).

Only when these two elements are clearly appre-
hended as complementary, not as exclusive, are we assured of a sound concept of revelation. The world of
reality and the world of value-judgments are not two
but indissolubly one. To think otherwise has been the
error of the theology dominated by the critical Kantian
philosophy. In these systems, revelation has been ille-
gitimately bifurcated. This may not be done, for without a genuine divine revelation in nature, history, and
conscience, the so-called special revelation of super-

natural spiritual truths loses contact with the whole
of cosmic reality. And if, as a consequence, the essence of religion is sought in the "practical reason"
(Kant) or in a *donum superadditum* (Catholicism), in
each case religion comes to stand alongside of common
human existence in an artificial manner. It appears
as a sectarian phenomenon, and its totalitarian claim is
gone. On the contrary, only a theistic monism can
guarantee a sound philosophy of revelation. Such a
view is not only cosmic in sweep but unifying as well.
And so Bavinck concludes his discussion of revelation
with these magnificent words:

"It can therefore be the purpose of revelation not only to
teach man and to enlighten his reason (Rationalism), to cause
him to conduct himself virtuously (Moralism), to awaken in
him religious sentiments (Mysticism). But God's purpose in
His special revelation penetrates much deeper, and has a much
broader extent. It is none other than to wrest man from the
power of sin and to cause the glory of God to beam forth
again from all creatures. And this has reference to man in
his entirety, including body and soul and all his capacities and
powers. Nor does it comprehend only a few isolated humans
but humanity as an organic whole. And finally, it takes in
not only humanity apart from other creatures, but heaven
and earth as well—in short, the whole world in its organic
existence. Sin has spoiled and devastated everything, reason
and will, the ethical and physical world. Consequently in
his work of rescue and restoration God concerns Himself with
the whole of humanity and the whole cosmos. Most certainly
God's revelation is soteriological, but the object of that salvation is the cosmos, and not only the ethical part of man,
or his will in abstraction from his reason, nor the psychical
apart from the physical, but everything together. 'For God hath
shut up all unto disobedience, that He might have mercy on
all'" (*op. cit.* vol. I, p. 318).

All natural human organs may serve as tools for
the transmission of revelation because they have been

created for that purpose and fulfill their true function
only when so used. In the sacramental view of life
which we are advocating, there is nothing common or
unclean. All things have been made to serve the divine
purpose of self-disclosure or revelation. In Him all
things beget their meaning and true fulfillment but only
when linked with Him, not when unnaturally divorced
from Him. In isolation from the revealed Deity, it is
not proper or possible to speak of any created thing as
a revelation, for there is nothing there to be revealed.
The content of revelation is always divine, and the
divine, though manifested through natural media, is
always essentially supernatural.

The single issue to which a careful study of the concept of revelation leads is the discovery of the fatal
fallacy of divorcing the subjective and the objective in
revelation. The necessity of maintaining a conjunction
of these two elements is the perennial obligation of the
Christian Church. Failing this, we shall have a warped,
and therefore untrue conception of that which constitutes the very essence of religion and of Christianity in
particular. For religion is bound up with the idea of
revelation. But religion, even in its crudest forms, as-
sumes the existence of a different order, which we cannot know unless it is revealed. The holy One, Who is
enthroned above, is known also as the pervading presence in the world around us. He is at once the majesty
in the heavens, Whom men are to worship with infinite
awe, and a God near us, with Whom we can hold the
closest communion. Both conceptions are necessary, and
a grave danger arises when they are kept separate.
When all stress is laid on God's transcendence, as in
Barthianism, He becomes unreal and remote. When He
becomes purely immanent, as He was conceived in the

period from Lessing to Barth, we have the pantheistic confusion of God with moral achievements and with enthusiasm for scientific research (as in Lessing), or with a mystical absorption of the soul into itself or into the All (as in Schleiermacher), or with the release of values and ideals inherent in man's moral nature (as in Ritschlianism). Instead of this unnatural severance, the two conceptions must go together. They are but two different modes of apprehending the same reality, which is at once the ground of all being and yet stands apart from it as that which is revealed. Nothing suffices but a theistical-monistic view when it comes to this central theological doctrine of revelation.

It has been our contention, this morning that the barrenness and sterility we experience today, both in the field of philosophy, as such, and in the domain of religious philosophy or theology, is due to an unnatural severance of what God intends to be together: man's religious faith, his scientific pursuits, and his aesthetic appreciations. The severance of any one of these from the other, after the fashion that Professor T. V. Smith undertakes it, is the perennial danger against which we must be on our guard in the field of general culture. And, as Calvinists who believe in the sovereignty of God, we have a heavy responsibility in this very regard. The same is true in the more strictly theological realm, as we tried to point out in reference to the concept of revelation. The call of the hour is for the maintenance of balance, in keeping together the conception of the lordship of God and the reality of His historic manifestations, on the one hand, and His indwelling presence in the world and in the heart of man on the other.

AND ETHICS

THE REV. WM. MATHESON

THE SCRIPTURE doctrine of the sovereignty of God implicates the fact of creation. God alone is from ever-lasting to everlasting. "All things were made by him; and without him was not anything made that was made" (John 1:3). He is, therefore, sovereign Lord of all. "Everything that being hath His kingdom doth command" (Ps. 103:19). In the interrelations of moral agents and God in which free agency on the part of the created as of the Creator is involved, this sovereignty of God is untrammeled. Of His own will and, there-fore, of His own sovereignty, all created beings exist and are constituted as they are. "The gifts and callings of God are without repentance" (Rom. 11:29), but only in accordance with His sovereign purpose were these gifts bestowed and are they enjoyed and exercised.

The sovereignty of God, therefore, involves that there is nothing beyond His will that in any wise limits Him, while on the other hand all that is created and is thus objective to Him is limited by His will. If we think of limitation in face of rebellion in His universe, we must think of His will prior to it all and of the fact that the gifts and calling of God are without repentance, so that "He is in one mind, and who can turn him?" (Job

23:13). This is expressed in Isaiah (40: 13-18): "Who hath directed the Spirit of the LORD, or being his counsellor hath taught him? With whom took he counsel, and who instructed him, and taught him in the path of judgment, and taught him knowledge, and showed to him the way of understanding? . . . All nations before him are as nothing . . . and vanity. To whom then will ye liken God?" It is taken up in Paul's Epistle to the Romans after dealing with the problem of Israel's falling away through unbelief (11: 33-36): "O the depth of the riches both of the wisdom and knowledge of God! how unsearchable are his judgments, and his ways past finding out! For who hath known the mind of the Lord? or who hath been his counsellor? or who hath first given to him, and it shall be recompensed unto him again? For of him, and through him, and to him, are all things: to whom be glory forever. Amen." In what to us remain the unfathomable depths of our spiritual beings whence the exercise of free agency turns to conflict with the will of God, the full sovereignty of God never relaxes. And of this incomparable inscrutably penetrating sovereignty it is that Jesus teaches when, having upbraided the cities wherein most of His mighty works were done because they repented not, He turned in adoring love and calmly acquiescent restfulness of spirit to the Father, saying, "I thank thee, O Father, Lord of heaven and earth, because thou hast hid these things from the wise and prudent, and hast revealed them unto babes. Even so, Father, for so it seemed good in thy sight."

There is something in that sovereignty to be known that brings this joyous peace to the heart and full satisfaction to the understanding. For Jesus continues to explain: "All things are delivered unto me of my

Father: and no man knoweth the Son but the Father; neither knoweth any man the Father save the Son and he to whomsoever the Son will reveal him"; and as showing forth the very purpose of His coming into the world and His will to reveal the Father, He says, "Come unto me, all ye that labor and are heaven laden, and I will give you rest." He willeth to give knowledge of the Father to all who labor and are heavy laden. In this knowledge of the Father, rest is found. The knowledge of the Father reveals the true character of His sovereignty.

The sovereignty of God is not then to be imagined as a merely arbitrary exercise of irresistible power. It is true that God gives account to no one of any of His matters. There is no higher authority to which He defers. He doeth His own will in the army of heaven and among the inhabitants of the earth. It is true that He makes all things work together according to the counsel of His own will and that He alone is, therefore, the absolute arbiter of the final issue in all things and that in being so He sets bounds even unto the remnant of man's wrath. Nothing is too small to escape His notice, control, and direction, nor is anything so great or so mighty as to withstand His will. Yet is it true that His will is the expression of His character and that His character is of such an order that He can and does say to men, "Come now, and let us reason together."

In regard to the overthrow of Sodom and Gomorrah and to Abraham's interest there, God records Himself as saying of Abraham, "For I know him, that he will command his children and his household after him, and they shall keep the way of the LORD, to do justice and judgment." So the way of Jehovah is simply to do justice and judgment. After He revealed to Abraham

His purpose of inquiry in order to the execution of judgment against the cities of the plain for their iniquities, Abraham pleaded with the Lord, "Wilt thou also destroy the righteous with the wicked? . . . That be far from thee to do after this manner to slay the righteous with the wicked: Shall not the Judge of all the earth do right?" And to this appeal and plea, Jehovah lent His ear.

This illustrates the point in hand. It is impossible for God in the exercise of His sovereignty to deal unjustly with any of His creatures. The way of the Lord is always to do justice and judgment, for all His works are truth and His ways judgment, as Nebuchadnezzar had to testify. God is just and of Him it is true that, "if we believe not, yet he abideth faithful: he cannot deny himself." It is this element in the character of God to which John refers when he says of the commission Jesus gave to His disciples, "This then is the message which we have heard of him and declare unto you, That God is light and in him is no darkness at all." Without an appreciation of this revelation of the Father by the Son, that He is just, ever and forever just, there can be no true appreciation of any phase of the teaching of Jesus. This is the foundation principle of God's revelation of Himself, just as John stresses it: "This then is the message which we have heard of him and declare unto you." Within the bounds of justice all is light, but all is dark without.

In the Epistle of James, this is set before us as the foundation principle of the moral law, "If ye fulfil the royal law according to the Scriptures, Thou shalt love thy neighbor as thyself, ye do well: but if ye have respect to persons ye commit sin, and are convinced of the law as transgressors." In like manner, David declares, "The Spirit of God spake by me, and his word was in my tongue. The God of Israel said, the Rock of Israel spake unto me, He that ruleth over men must be just, ruling in the fear of God." All unjust dealing conflicts with reverence for the living God. So is proclaimed in the Law of Moses and repeatedly declared of God in Scriptures, Old and New, that there is no respect to persons with Him. It is this ethical principle that underlies the Ten Commandments and that reveals itself in the faithfulness of God so largely unfolded in the Psalms, the Songs of His praise. Simply because He is faithful, just, true, He is to be trusted, for the ground of trust is truth. So in full and lively recognition of His sovereignty, sinners are welcome to reason with Him and to make appeal to His Self-revealed character as a just God and a Savior.

But God's sovereignty is quite freely and fully revealed to be the sovereignty of love. Justice sets the lines to all right action, and love it is that moves within those lines to all righteousness. And God is love. The urge of all revelation is directed to this point as clearly and insistently as it is directed to the unswerving justness of God. This cannot be better illustrated than in His reasoning with Cain. The Lord insisted that in His acceptance of Abel's offering as over against His rejection of Cain's there was no respect to persons and that still the way of acceptance was open to Cain and at hand. It shines forth in the week's respite to the impenitent because of unbelieving victims of the flood in the time of Noah. It comes to vehement expression in Ezekiel, the prophet of God's justness: "As I live, saith the LORD, I have no pleasure in the death of the wicked, but that the wicked turn from his way and live: turn ye, turn ye, from your evil ways; for why will ye die, O house of

Israel?" When Jesus dealt with Nicodemus, startling
him with the statement of the necessity of the new birth
in order to an understanding of the things of God and
to entrance into the kingdom of God, yet leading him
deeply into the mystery of the sovereignty of the Holy
Spirit's operation in the matter, it was to this great
fact of God's character He led him: "For God so loved
the world that he gave his only begotten Son that whosoever believeth in him should not perish but have everlasting life."

The principle of ethical behavior is justice. Its motive power is love. Justice is the principle of order in
the society of righteous free agents. Love is the bond
of its unity. From this it is clear that the sovereignty
of God is to be conceived of as supremely ethical in
character. However profound the mystery of His overruling Providence must always appear to us, and especially under conditions of severe and threateningly
overwhelming temptation and trial, we are ever to bear
in mind that He is just in all His ways and works and
ever moves in love; that anyone should be wronged by
His sovereign appointments is simply an impossibility.
True, in a world whereinto sin, which is fundamental injustice, has entered, men do suffer ghastly wrongs at the
hands of their fellow-men, but this is, after all, simply
the outworking of the curse of justice upon transgres-
sion in which we all are involved. And, furthermore,
in our judgments of things we know only in part and
that part is colored by personal bias. Despite the fact
of injustice so marked in the experiences of men, the
glory of God's sovereignty in its supremely ethical
character emerges in His overruling all in such wise
that the victory rests with justice in the end to the eternal praise of His love. To reflect this divine ethical

character in his dominion over the creatures of this earth, man was constituted. Fallen and become the object of the supreme exhibition of God's justice and love in his redemption, man is called to reflect anew and with incomparably increased power this perfection of moral character. "I am come," said Jesus Christ, "that they might have life, and that they might have it more abundantly" (John 10:10), and so we read His words, "Ye have heard that it hath been said, Thou shalt love thy neighbor, and hate thine enemy. But I say unto you, Love your enemies, bless them that curse you, do good to them that hate you, and pray for them which despitefully use you, and persecute you; that ye may be the children of your Father which is in heaven: for he maketh his sun to rise on the evil and on the good, and sendeth rain on the just and on the unjust. For if ye love them which love you, what reward have ye? Do not even the publicans the same? And if ye salute your brethren only, what do ye more than others? do not even the publicans so? Be ye therefore perfect, even as your Father which is in heaven is perfect." The truly ethical in man is thus the reflection of the ethical which supremely characterizes the sovereignty of God and is reflected in man through man's knowledge of God. And so may we understand the sublime words of Paul's Second Epistle to the Corinthians (3:18): "But we all, with open face beholding as in a glass the glory of the Lord, are changed into the same image from glory to glory, even as by the Spirit of the Lord."

And so when Jesus was asked, "Master, which is the great commandment in the law?" He replied in practically identical words with those of the lawyer who asked Him, "Master, what shall I do to inherit eternal life?" only to have his question turned back for answer from himself. And he, answering, said, "Thou shalt love the Lord thy God with all thy heart, and with all thy soul, and with all thy strength and with all thy mind; and thy neighbor as thyself." Now, Jesus gave priority to the first as the greatest but declared the second to be like the first. Then He added, "On these two commandments hang all the law and the prophets." The first commandment defines the true religion. The second commandment defines the true ethic. The first commandment reveals true religion as joyous and unre-served acquiescence in the sovereignty of God, and out of that issues the fruit of ethical conduct in relation to the world, to our fellow-creatures, and to human society. This conduct, being the reflection in man of the ethical character of the sovereignty of God, col-laborates in perfect unison with the divine will and, being the free expression of the inmost being, moves in the sphere and in the atmosphere of perfect freedom.

In this answer of Jesus to the lawyer's question, "Master, which is the great commandment in the law?" we have impressively set before us the fact that the truly ethical life has its roots in the religious life and that the truly religious life of unreserved acquiescence and joyous glorying in the sovereignty of God. Plainly, it is implicated that without obedience to the first and great commandment, obedience to the second must fail. As like begets like, so the second is begotten of the first. Without the first, we cannot have the second: without the great, we cannot have the less. And the first and great commandment postulates the absolute sovereignty of God. To Him we owe unreserved and whole-hearted surrender in love from the inmost deeps of our being to the outmost fringes of our activity. Given that the

second, of necessity, follows, even to love our neighbor
as ourselves. This reveals the vital nexus between that
worship of God which glories in His sovereignty and
that keeping of His way which rejoices in our neighbor's welfare as in our own. And so Jesus declared,
"On these two commandments hang all the law and the
prophets." In these two commandments are summed up
the principles of true religion and morality, and in
their juxtaposition by Jesus is set forth the vital connection between the sovereignty of God and ethics. It
is interesting to observe how these two are conjoined
in the Fourth Commandment in which man's way of
observing the Sabbath rest is patterned upon God's way
of work and rest and yet is insisted upon as meeting
the creaturely need of rest.

A brief analysis of the command, "Thou shalt love
thy neighbor as thyself," is now in order. To get at
the underlying factor in this rule of life, we may omit
the words, "thy neighbor as." These words introduce
us into the special sphere of personal relationships.
They introduce "the other." We read the command,
then, for purposes of analysis, "Thou shalt love . . .
thyself." This is the starting point in this Second Commandment. So it appears in the Golden Rule: "Whatsoever ye would that men should do unto you, do ye
even so unto them." This principle of self-love that is
here enunciated is of primary importance. It is a wholly
unscriptural mode of expression that is used when men
speak of being "selfless." It is a meaningless sham and
is in open conflict with all righteousness. Even in the
abandon of the soul's surrender to God in obedience to
the first and great commandment, it would be quite
untrue to speak of the soul as selfless. In that surrender
there is no hint of the merging of ourselves in God.

There abides the consciousness of God as objective to oneself and of oneself as objective to God — there is, therefore, joy unspeakable and full of glory. Much less, then, is there any room for such an ideal as one's becoming selfless in the presence of any creature. The basic principle of the Scripture ethic is self-love. It is in the ignoring of this and in the consequent failure to give due place to the principle of justice that altruism becomes defective.

The perfection of God's sovereignty is displayed in that He made this world a perfect place for man's dwelling. For every possible need of man's complex constitution, provision was made in the world in which God placed him and to every provision in the world as constituted by God there is a corresponding requirement, possible need or power of enjoyment in man's nature. It is true that man has lost control or dominion over the creatures with which God has furnished him. It is true that man now abuses God's best gifts by excess and misuse. It is true that men often become the slaves of their own appetites or tastes for food and drink and other means of gratification. It is true that men, staggering under enslavement to such appetites, in anguish turn upon the gifts of God to denounce them as vile and to declare that this world would be better without them. But this is for man to excuse himself by denying the very nature that God gave him because he has lost control over his own natural and perfectly ethical appetites and tastes through cutting himself off from God in rebellion. This is the essence of hypocrisy and the acme of the climax of ethical degeneracy. Excess in the use of the creature is simply contrary to the dictate of God's law, "Thou shalt love thyself." It is to become the slave of the creature God created to be at

man's command, and privation is simply the opposite
extreme. The way of use without abuse is the way of
Jesus, the Messiah.

Having observed that the free and controlled enjoyment of all good things provided in God's sovereignty
for man and that "every creature of God is good, and
nothing to be refused, if it be received with thanksgiving," is the dictate of the law, "Thou shalt love thyself," with respect to the use of things, we come to the
question of man's securing his living. It is not without
God's sovereign design that anyone is in the world. This
being so, it were a reflection upon God's sovereignty
that the means of living should not normally be present
in the world. God's judgment against a people for their
iniquities may take the form of depriving them of the
necessities of life, but God has ordained that there
should normally be provided a living for those who
under His sovereign control enter upon the stage of this
world's activities. But is it true, as many affirm, that
"this world owes man his living"? There is a living
provided for man in this world, but man must labor
and toil to get his living and the living of those dependent upon him. That is a fundamental principle.
Under the discipline of God's sovereign direction, fallen
man must remember God's Word: "In the sweat of thy
face thou shalt eat bread." Man is to love himself.
That love is to express itself in his toil for the necessities of life for himself and for those for whom he is
responsible. What he may be able to secure above that
is wholly secondary and it is not for such he toils. It
is contrary to the ethics of Scripture and in open defiance of the sovereignty of God that men should seek
to be maintained in idleness by the labors of others
rather than toil for their own bread, whether through

idleness or under the pretext that they are not able to secure a surplus above their living in return for their labors. So it is declared by the Holy Spirit in Paul in his Second Epistle to the Thessalonians: "For even when we were with you, this we commanded you, that if any would not work, neither should he eat." This seems to be the force of God's Word in the Fourth Commandment: "Six days shalt thou labor and do all thy work."

There can be no prospect of ethical or moral development without the hearty recognition of the personal responsibility involved in the command, "Thou shalt love thyself." Every scheme of so-called moral reform which condones failure by placing responsibility for it on objective conditions conflicts with a full recognition of personal responsibility, reflects on the sovereignty of God and is ethically fatal. It is quite clear that the rule of self-love as manifested in the labor of winning one's living and in the activity of enjoying the good things with which God has filled this earth for the use of man is the way that lies between excess and privation. That regard for God's sovereignty which manifests itself in thanksgiving spells balance or control in the practical enjoyment of what He gives. Thus the fully rounded enjoyment of the good things of this life with thanksgiving to God is the highest ethical attainment in this sphere of the ethical life. Asceticism has no place in the Christian ethic. The place of fasting belongs only to the discipline that aims at true control or, it may be, springs from intensity of spiritual desire or emotion. In holding true the balance between privation and excess, the rule of justice, which more clearly emerges in personal relations, is displayed. That rule of justice or "no respect to persons" is simply stated, "thy neigh-bor as thyself."

Love is the motive power in all right action. But love is not a law, neither does love define a law. "Love is the fulfilling of the law." The law is simply the dictate of justice. Therefore, "Love rejoices not in iniquity but rejoices in the truth." Here the truth is set over against iniquity, and the identity between the law of truth and the law of justice is proclaimed. The truth may be defined as justice to the facts. There arises here the old question whether it can ever be right or truly ethical to tell a lie. Sometimes it may appear that love to a friend may urge against telling the truth and to speaking untruth: that love or loyalty to an or-ganization, as the church, may urge to the perversion of facts, the declaring that facts are or were not just as in reality they are or were. In this way love and truth are made to appear as in conflict. Now, as love belongs to the emotional or subjective and truth belongs to the objective, no such conflict is possible just as it is implied in the statement quoted, "Love rejoiceth not in iniquity, but rejoiceth in the truth." That is not love which urges to untruth. There enters another ele-ment where that urge is present. That other factor in-volves the notion of expediency, which implies the exer-cise of judgment. But reality or facts as actually existent is to be recognized as developed under the sovereignty of God. To quarrel with this or to attempt to make it appear other than it is, is to assail the sover-eignty of God. The law that love fulfils, then, must ever be the law of truth, and so our Lord, speaking of His kingdom to Pilate, said, "Everyone who is of the truth heareth my voice."

Perhaps it is here, too, that we should deal with

gambling, not in the manifoldness of its ramifications nor in the insidiousness and subtlety of its pervasiveness, but in the ethical principle involved. I take it that gambling as distinguished from mere speculation is the investing of something with a view to receiving a return that depends upon the unknown development of a mere event as over against a return that depends upon the unknown development of a natural resource. In the one case the investment has no causal or fructifying connection with the return expected. In the other case there is such a relation. In the one case there is no ground in justice for the expectation of a return, whereas in the other case there is. In the one case the sovereignty of God in Providence is prostituted to the end of unjust gain through man's ignorance of the unrevealed future. In the other case the sovereignty of God in Providence may be relied upon with a confidence born of the recognition of the nature of His sovereignty as exercised in justice.

That which places any action or activity outside the pale of the ethical is simply whatsoever there is about it that bears the character of injustice or untruth. In the sphere of personal relations, the bearing of this rule of "thy neighbor as thyself" cannot possibly be better interpreted nor more clearly illustrated than in the story that has come to bear the title of "The Good Samaritan." Jesus was asked, "Master, what shall I do to inherit eternal life?" and to this He replied, "What is written in the law? How readest thou?" In the story of the Samaritan, Jesus expressly set forth the requirement of justice. The stricken victim of the thieves received at the Samaritan's hand only what the law required when it dictated, "Thou shalt love thy neighbor as thyself." The priest and the Levite flouted the authority

of the law of that very religion they professed. The
Samaritan rose to the occasion. Separated as he was
from this Jew who, by what men would call an awkward
chance, had become neighbor to him, on the score of
religion, of race, of language, of circle of acquaintance,
of place of residence, of apparent social and economic
status, there remained merely the bond of their common humanity between them. Yet the Samaritan, mani-
festly on an urgent errand, saw it to be his duty to
delay his progress to aid this victim of violence for
which he was in no wise himself responsible. He did
for this stranger, who in God's sovereign appointment
unexpectedly became neighbor to him, just as he would
have another do for himself. He did not one whit more
than what justice, or "no respect to persons," required
of him. It is plainly to pervert the teaching of our Lord
here to interpret the Samaritan's action as in any aspect
a manifestation of grace. Jesus was dealing explicitly
with the interpretation of the law. Only as we appreciate this can we rise to conceive of the sovereignty of
God aright and sense the character or nature of the
principle of order and the bond of unity which constituted the human family one.

In the commandments, we find this principle of justice or truth applied to the various spheres of human
relationships in the order of vital interest. At the foundation lies the obligation owing to those from whom
we derive life—father and mother. Behind that lies the
marriage bond—twain in one—the true unit in human
society, holding its bond. Next comes the obligation
on account of life itself. Then follows the obligation
respecting the power of begetting life. The obligation
respecting the economic conditions and the social conditions of life complete this sphere of law bearing on

the purely human. The Tenth Commandment completes
the circle of the law by bringing us back to the first,
for covetousness is idolatry; "Ye cannot serve God and
mammon." Therefore are they declared to be of a corrupt and disputatious mind, destitute of the truth, whose
way of reckoning is that the way of gain is godliness
(I Tim. 6:5).

Justice is the bond that binds the conscience of man.
So in all systems of ethics, it receives a place. But in
the ethics of the Scripture appears a twofold divergence.
Here justice is revealed to be the basic principle of
right conduct. No urge of expediency, however press-
ing, can be allowed sway. Justice is simply as sacred
as God Himself, Who is the fountain and norm of
justice. Furthermore, the conception of the requirement
of justice penetrates here more deeply and carries
obligation far beyond what is elsewhere recognized. As
the principle of law, it defines and defends true
freedom.

But within the bounds of justice, there is wide scope
for the sway of love. In His Parable of the Laborers
in the Vineyard, Jesus may no doubt be taken to indicate that just treatment of a servant takes account of
the necessity of his having a living in reward for his
labors, without, of course, in any wise infringing upon
the principle that men are to eat their bread in the
sweat of their faces. But He clearly indicates that good-
will which is the expression of love has liberty "to do
what I will with mine own." This is the sphere of expediency that must live forever within the bounds of
justice. But the expediency of the Christian ethic ever
has respect to the necessity and the benefit of others.
This is the mind to which we are called in the Epistle
to the Philippians: "Let this mind be in you which was

also in Christ Jesus," the mind, "Think not every man on his own things but every man also on the things of others." It is one of the perversions of interpretation of this passage that it should be held to teach that Christian principles encourage the invasion of the liberty of any who do not abuse their liberty in order to help those who do abuse their liberty or to seek protection of society against such abuse. We cannot think on the things of others when we rob them of their liberty. In other words, there is no conflict here with the basic principle, "thy neighbor as thyself." It is our personal right or privilege to give up in love all we will for the benefit of our fellow-men. It is never our right or privilege according to the ethics of Christ to attempt to take from another for any cause that which is properly his. That is the high point in the ethics of the Christian—to rejoice in others' enjoying full freedom to do as they will with what is properly their own whilst ever rejoicing in doing with his own whatsoever lies in his power for the benefit of others. It is the very urge of love that "It is more blessed to give than to receive," and so Paul declares with respect to meat offered in sacrifice to idols, "If meat make my brother to offend, I will eat no meat while the world stands lest I make my brother to offend." It was not his, however, to say even to fellow Christians: "Ye shall eat no meat lest ye make a brother to offend." To do that were to dishonor the sovereignty of God, Who reigns forever "with no respect to persons."

The sovereignty of God is the foundation principle of our Christian faith. The supremely ethical character of God's sovereignty belongs to its very essence. To reflect that character was man made "in the image and after the likeness of God." In the worship of God as sovereign Lord resides the power to reflect that character. The full display of God's character and so of the character as of the fact of His sovereignty emerges at the virgin birth, at the cross of Calvary, and the empty tomb. Accordingly, as therefore we glory in the sovereignty of God in the light of the knowledge of His glory which is His moral character revealed in Christ crucified, we must reflect that character in our own and so in our personal conduct. This, not mere economic and social regulation, is the hope of a sadly disorganized world. God speed the day when "the earth shall be filled with the knowledge of the glory of the LORD as the waters cover the sea."

PUBLIC ADDRESSES

AND AMERICAN ATTITUDES

PROF. DR. WM. ROBINSON

In a recent volume, a popular theologian laments that in America, Calvinism "perished suddenly, far too suddenly to yield up its eternal message." [1] This gathering is a concrete evidence that Calvinism has not perished in America. And it seems peculiarly appropriate that the descendants of those who made Holland a gracious haven for such Calvinsts as the Pilgrim Fathers and John Robinson, who argued against Arminius at the University of Leyden, should offer the environs of what was once New Amsterdam to initiate this movement. The European Calvinistic Congresses, beginning with the coming together of the British and Dutch Calvinists, have gone from strength unto strength in the Lord. As one who by name and connection comes from the Puritan and Presbyterian traditions, I thankfully accept this gracious hospitality of the Reformed Churches as an omen and a promise of a movement that God, in His wisdom, may see fit to use to call America into a living consciousness of His sovereign glory.

The Reformed Faith is the proclamation that the Lord God omnipotent reigneth, King of kings and Lord of

[1] Horton, **Contemporary Continental Theology**, p. 214

147

lords. Calvinism is a vision of God in all His glory, of the King in His beauty, and a consequent sense of our absolute dependence on Him. We depend upon Him for knowledge and recognize the sovereign authority of His revelation. We depend upon Him for life and history, believing that the almighty God governs the works of His hands and that in Christ He has supernaturally intervened for our salvation. Thus Christian theism is the statement of divine sovereignty. Taking seriously man's fallen condition and his need for a new relation, a new birth, and a new revelation, we depend upon the sovereign God for religion and for grace. Accordingly, "the Reformed Faith conceives itself as the most pure Biblicalism, theism, religion and grace" (C. W. Hodge, Jr.).

Over against Calvinism, there is an American instrumentalism which brings to our shores the humanism and agnosticism of Buddha, Confucius, Protagoras, and Comte. This attitude is distinctively subjective, denying the objectivity of truth, value, logic, aesthetics, and moral standards. For this Americanism, man occupies the first place, the judgment-seat; and, confident of his own sufficiency, asks whether there be a God or a revelation. For Calvinism, God and His revelation occupies the first place as a fundamentally established, objective, massive fact, which has its right in itself and does not need to be legitimized by man's vote. For American agnosticism, the question is: How can I know that God is? For the Calvinist, Jonathan Edwards, as for the Reformer Luther, the question is: "How can I gain a *gracious* God?"[2] For the former the problem is: What do I, in my fancied autonomy, absoluteness, and self-sufficiency think of God? And all too often the answer

---

[2] Koehler, W., **Dogmengeschichte**, 1938, pp. 351-352

to such human conceits is the decision of the classic humanist, Protagoras: "Concerning the gods I am unable to say whether they exist or not, nor if they do what they are like." For Calvinism, the query of an agonized conscience is: What does the Holy One of Israel think of me? And in the past, when that question was pressed upon the heart by the Holy Spirit, it became the forerunner of the Reformation and of the Great Awakening.

In cutting itself off from God and His objective revelation, American humanism has cut itself off from any permanent standard or abiding truth. Personal guesses at ultimate reality take the place of eternal truth. Conceptions of truth, goodness, and beauty become mere hypotheses, "intellectual instruments to be tested and confirmed — and altered — through consequences effected by acting upon them."[3] Knowledge no longer relates to that which has antecedent existence or essential being; but "all knowing, judgment, belief represents an acquired result of the working of natural impulses in connection with environment."[4] Instrumentalism takes the place of logic as expediency supplants principle; and "that theory is 'true' which corresponds most effectively to the needs of society at any given moment." Instrumentalism is a formula for the way in which men respond when specific conditions present themselves. Its sole authority is expediency, its sole test success. For to it "the good is never twice alike. It never copies itself. It is new every morning and fresh every evening."[5] And again, "every truth has its day. But this does not matter so long as sufficient for the

[3] Dewey, John, **The Quest for Certainty**, p. 264
[4] Dewey, John, **Human Nature and Conduct**, p. 211
[5] **Op. cit.**, p. 211

day is the truth thereof." Even order, unity, and con-
tinuity are treated as human inventions. Accordingly,
there is no right and wrong, no true and false, no ultimate law of contradiction, no eternal ideals or norms.

Instrumentalism is not limited to the overt humanists,
but may often be found in the thinking of those who are
ecclesiastically far from humanism. According to it,
the position which one takes in one instance need not
be repeated in another. Thus, one may tolerate "liberal"
nullifiers of the Five Points of the General Assembly
while one "cracks down" on conservatives who disobey
other orders of the Assembly. One may become furious
at the temper of conservative criticism of modernistic
action, while his own "liberal" "sweetness and light"
express themselves in caricaturing the conservative viewpoint and in treating their representatives with sarcasm.
The same findings measured Schofield by the Westminster Standards and quite properly condemned certain features of his dispensationalism; and, then, im-
properly, measured Schleiermacher by a pragmatic test
and commended the father of modernism. All of which
is diametrically contrary to the Word which declares,

> *Diverse weights and diverse measures,*
> *Both of them alike are an abomination to Jehovah.*

Over against this American attitude, Calvinism lifts
the banner of God's Word. Realizing that we are finite,
sin-blinded, and immature, we look to God for light.
Lacking wisdom, we ask of God. We do not consider
our reasons as an autonomous power, but a gift of God
which must always remain subject to His revelation. We
strive for His glory through unconditioned subjection
to His Word as against all human commands. In knowledge, as in life, we live out of the Father hand of God.

The Father knoweth all things in knowing completely the Son; the Son knows all things, especially His sheep, in knowing completely the Father (Matt. 11:27; John 10:14); and the Spirit knoweth even the deep things of God (John 15: 13-15; I Cor. 1:11). Thus the counsels of the Trinity span all reality and our task is to reinterpret what God hath preinterpreted—to think God's thoughts after Him. The decrees of God are the plan of the ages, the warp and woof of history, on which by the light of His Word we are to trace the triumphs of our God.

That Word tells us that all things visible and invisible were created in Christ (Col. 1:16); accordingly the Nicene Creed confesses God as the creator of all things visible and invisible. In distinction from Kantianism, which is sweeping much of current European theology, Augustinianism insists that the universals of knowledge come not from fallen, depraved man, but from God. And because they do, there are universal truths, eternal ideals, common denominators, by which we are able to converse and write in a way that others can understand. Because God is and the principles by which we are capable of knowing anything have their foundation in Him, language, logic, mathematics, and science are possible.

With "Rabbi" Duncan, the beloved Scottish divine, Calvinism recovers its philosophical faith on a theological basis. "If we do not assume God, and reason downwards, I doubt we shall ever rise to Him at all. Once a man has said his 'credo,' and especially if his creed has been christened, he may build his philosophy as high as heaven. The tendency of all my thinking is not to look upwards from man to God, but downwards from God to man. . . . I find that I cannot bridge the gulf between the creature and a Creator, the many and the One, in my ascent, so I endeavor to do so in my descent. . . . You tell me that this or that is the voice of Nature, and that we can't help believing it. But does this Reidist solution really satisfy any man? The belief may be false though we cannot help believing it? May not some malign being, an evil demon, have created us, or such a demiourgos as the Gnostics believed in? Can't-help-myself-ism is to me a very shallow philosophy. But if I am 'made in the image of God,' my philosophy is underpropped by theology, and the truth of what my nature avers is guaranteed to me" (*Colloquia Peripatetica*, 1, 2). The simplest subject-object relation in empirical cognition implies the trustworthiness of the functioning of the senses, the validity of the intellectual concepts which interpret the sense data, and a true correlation between the knowing subject and the known object. But every item in this statement ultimately rests upon faith in the Creator of senses, conceptional reason, and the relativity of the knower and known. Accordingly, God is the ultimate of every bit of empirical or scientific knowledge.

When one has the privilege of visiting the Berry Schools and sees every arch framing a spire or notices the care and precision with which the youth of America are marshaled to enter the beautiful chapel, a replica of that one which Washington attended, he realizes that this beauty of architecture, this order of marching feet, the stimulus, thrill, and challenge of the whole undertaking, did not merely happen. There is thought, planning, aesthetic sensibility of the highest order—there is a House of Dreams and a great soul capable of altruistic and ennobling aspirations behind this great Georgia institution. How much more when we gaze at "the gray-black velvet of the sky on which a Master hand has flung His jewels for admiration"; when we watch the glowing tints of morning or the variegated colors of autumn, when we listen to the artless prattle of childhood, when we delve into the intricacies of the atom are we brought to the feet of our Creator, lost in wonder and admiration for His wisdom, the beauty of His holiness, and the order He hath ordained! We would acknowledge Him in all our ways and have Him direct our paths.

Accepting God as the ultimate and final truth means acknowledging His authority, yielding obedience to His will. The knowledge of God is no abstract entity but the obedience of faith. Our day has run riot in license and individualism, but the revolt of youth has spent itself and men are establishing everywhere some form of authoritarianism—Communism—Fascism—Nazism. Instead of the arbitrary commandments of men, Calvinism offers the wisdom of God—the wisdom of Him Who can no more fail to do good than He can fail to be. It is our duty to think God's thoughts after Him. But our first responsibility is not that our minds abstractly understand the complete coherence of the Creator's plan; but that our wills yield obedience to His commands. If any man will do His will, He shall know of the doctrine. We walk by faith, not by sight; and the obedience of faith is the way of knowledge. Calvinism stands for standards of truth, of right, of beauty, of value—for the authority of God in every life and all of life — for Jesus Christ as Lord of lords and King of kings — for the Scriptures of the Old and New Testaments as the only infallible rule of faith, worship, and life.

In particular, Calvinism as the most consistent and harmonious statement of Christianity, finds in the atoning cross of Christ a memorial to all generations of those eternal principles or rectitude which spring from God's essence and regulate all the decisions of His will. Even the good-news of His forgiving grace reveals His righteousness and shows that His wrath is revealed from heaven against all unrighteousness and ungodliness of men. God's power to save is a moral power. He saves not by destroying but by satisfying the claims of justice. The gospel is not a compromise with sin but a substitution; not a cancellation of the debt of sin, but its satisfaction; not a mere wiping off, but a wiping out in blood and agony and death. In my place, condemned He stood; sealed my pardon with His blood. The gospel shows that God is a just God and a Savior, and thereby establishes the justice of God, our Savior. The holy God can no more fail to punish sin than He can lie. Every sin will be adequately punished but, blessed be God, not every sinner. But the sinner who stoops in penitence and trembling faith before the Lamb of God who bore our sins in His own body on the tree realizes that justice was done on that hill without the city wall, that just wrath broke over our dear Savior, so that God is just when He justifies him that believes in Jesus. The law, the principles of truth, of right, and of justice are honorable; Christ honored them in satisfying their every claim. God declared that these eternal norms are emanations of His very essence when He so signally honored them in Gethsemane and Golgotha. Righteousness and truth were never so exalted as when, delighting to do the Father's will, Christ vindicated and exalted them. "Because thou hast loved righteousness and hated iniquity, therefore, O God, thy God, hath exalted thee." In dying to satisfy the just demands of the law and in being exalted for that love of righteousness,

Christ has declared to all men that righteousness and justice are the foundation of God's throne. May America heed the declaration of the cross rather than the siren voices of humanistic skepticism!

Against the current American attempt to present a God limited by the will of men and by the laws of nature, Calvinism presents the Lord of hosts, Who is sovereign over life, history, and nature.

The sovereignty of God rests in His self-existence. God exists of Himself and everything else exists of His will and power. God is the only one to whom the predicate of "being" is applicable in the full sense. Being is the very essence of God; for every creature to *be* means to have been created and to be upheld by God. The fundamental philosophy underlying the Scripture from Genesis through Revelation is just this distinction between the Creator and the creature. And this distinction is the foundation of the sovereignty of God. When the Madras Conference Message denied that God was "sufficient to Himself" it set itself against the fundamental doctrine of historic Christianity, Roman Catholic as well as Protestant. Both Professor Karl Adam of Tübingen, a Roman Catholic scholar, and Professor Valentine Hepp of Amsterdam, a Reformed theologian, declare that God is self-existent and sufficient unto Himself in the plentitude of His triune glory. Creation was not necessary to His blessedness or holiness or society; it was and is an act of God's free grace. Since He does exist of Himself, the triune God is sufficient for Himself and for His people and reigns over the works of His hands. Jehovah of hosts doeth His will in the armies of heaven and among the children of men. "The Lord God, omnipotent, reigneth."

The sovereignty of God over life and history is opposed by those who insist on single-line thinking. In the Orient, this single-line thinking more often, perhaps, takes the form of determinism or fatalism. Because God is the highest cause of everything that occurs it is assumed that He is the sole efficient cause; and when one has said that God is the cause of a certain event, it is assumed that man is excused for his responsibility therein. In certain forms of New England theology men came perilously near to making God the cause of sin in the same sense as He is the cause of creation. However, John Calvin taught that man fell solely by his own will, which had the full power of contrary choice; that we must distinguish between the secret and the revealed will of God and be governed by the latter; that God's plan requires us to use prudence, precautions, means, and remedies. In His infinite wisdom, God predestined and preserves the free agency and moral responsibility of men. There are more causes than one for every human action, and man is responsible for his causality in every case, however fully the great and gracious God may overrule our sinful acts for His own glory. Christ was taken and by wicked hands crucified and slain, though the sovereign God used that fearful crime for the salvation of souls and the manifestation of His glorious grace.

American thinking is more prone to run to another form of single-line thinking. Because we are finite and limited; because we are circumscribed on every side by nature and the wills of other persons; because we know not what a day may bring forth; therefore, we are prone to reason that God is likewise limited. A popular American philosopher describes God as limited by the will of man, by natural laws, by circumstances, by inertia in things, and by chance in events. A noted psychologist has described a finite God making a courageous fight against evil but likely to lose the battle unless we come to his aid. Others represent God as a mere part or process in nature, the growing good in our mutuality, a finite struggling being who grows by human compromises and social integrations. For Arminianism the decisions of men are beyond God's knowledge and plan; for naturalism the laws of nature are not subject to His authority. Frankly, there is little reason to believe in or to preach such a God. In the battle of life, there are emergencies with which He cannot cope. He can see little, if any, farther than we can. He may be the President of the republic of souls, but He needs our help as much as we need His, and must resort to fireside chats to bring us to the rescue of His "new deal." We must plan to meet the issues of life in our own spiritual and moral resources, for we have no assurance that His grace will be sufficient for our needs. Now, all this is just paganism.

Calvin taught a Biblical Christianity that recognized the infinite greatness of the highest cause. Recognizing that God's thoughts were not our thoughts, that the things that are hidden belong unto God and the things that are revealed belong unto us and our children, Calvin called for double-line thinking. From God's standpoint, everything is indubitably certain; from our standpoint every future event is uncertain and contingent. And things are certain for God, not by an absolute or natural necessity, not by the Stoic conception of a necessity arising from a perpetual concatenation and intricate series of causes contained in nature; but by the inscrutible plan and will of God. Nothing occurs but by God's appointment, but the mode of this ordering is chiefly concealed in the purpose of God.

That plan includes the phenomena of nature, the acts of men—unfallen, fallen, regenerated—the ministry of angels, the acts of demons, and perhaps other agencies that are not dreamed of in our philosophies. And the wisdom of the Most High is so great that every creature is dealt with according to his nature so that no violence is done to the will of the creature. The Judge of the whole earth does right to every man.

The same act may display the criminality of man and the overruling goodness of God. Joseph reminded his brethren that they meant their betrayal of him for evil but that God meant it for good. Thus the same event *in different aspects* may be agreeable to His secret and contrary to His revealed will. In crying for the shedding of Jesus' blood, the Jews were violating the revealed will of God and carrying out whatsoever His hand and secret counsel foreordained to come to pass. Thus God fulfills His righteous will at times even by the evil acts of evil men, but that in such a way that they are not inexcusable.

In considering any human event, we are called to run both the divine and the human line accurately through the event and carefully to avoid changing categories in the midst of the consideration. Forgetting this axiom, some Primitive Baptists have said that since God raised up Judas for the purpose which he fulfilled, therefore, he would be saved. But the Savior called Judas the "son of perdition" and said that it were better for him if he had not been born. The gospel story includes the treachery of Judas as definitely in the plan of God as the repentance of Peter. But the two events were in that plan in different ways. God permitted Judas to violate every principle of honor and continue his stubborn way in spite of every appeal of the Savior; while Jesus prayed for Peter that his faith might not fail and that he might be converted. All future things are uncertain for us; but God has given us His Word as the statement of His revealed will to regulate our lives. Seeking to observe that revelation, we can properly walk by faith, not by sight; for His everlasting and all-sufficient arms support our feeble steps.

Determinism teaches the single line of God's will and makes no provision for human responsibility; indeterminism offers a universe open for God as well as for man, like a train running head-on into the night with no hand at the throttle. Calvinism presents Biblical theism, in which God's plan includes the events that are to be as definite as those that are past, and which by shrouding the future from us preserves our moral responsibility and free agency and teaches us to walk by faith, not by sight. The story of Paul's shipwreck is a clear evidence that such faith in Providence does not produce inactivity. The Roman soldiers and Greek sailors, having no hope in a sufficient God, fasted in despondency; the Apostle, with hope in God, counseled food and took action. Faith in God's fatherly providence brings gratitude in prosperity, fortitude and patience in adversity, security in days of anxiety. A vision of the goodness of our God leads to repentance; and a knowledge that He can and will rule and overrule for our good, promotes charity toward those who have done us ill.

Then we also have in American universities an unmistakable tendency to deny the supernatural. For a man really to believe the miracles of the New Testament is tantamount to surrendering his academic standing. One of the roots of such thinking is the assumption that there has been no fall of man and that since the tree of life has continually advanced through the progress of the ages, there has been no need for supernatural intervention. It is said that God made things good enough in the beginning and does not need to intervene in the work of His hands. In place of the unique incarnation, expiation, resurrection, and ascension of our Lord, men decode these miraculous events into general truths and either present Jesus as one of the many mediators of men, one of the incarnations of Rama, or as an illustration of some general principle. The result is either comparative religion— Syncretism or Platonism, or else *Re-thinking Missions*— a combination of both these errors.

Christianity declares that man sinned and fell from the good estate in which God made him and that the Almighty God, the gracious God, did intervene in a miraculous way to save him. "For God so loved the world that He gave His only begotten Son that whosoever believeth on Him should not perish, but have everlasting life." God called the things that were not into being (Rom. 4:17). The Creator of all things visible and invisible can intervene in the order of nature; for nature is just God's usual mode of working. God's hands were not tied by the order He established and His heart was not hardened by our sin and iniquity. God, our Savior, did intervene, blessed be His name!

Calvinistic churches have properly sought to preserve the unique supernaturalism of the Christian faith against the onslaughts of naturalism. A platonic religion of general truths might be a good religion for angels; but Americans need the gospel that Christ died for our sins according to the Scriptures and rose again the third day according to the Scriptures. To preserve such truths, the General Assembly of the Presbyterian Church in the United States of America has thrice declared that "it is an essential doctrine of the Word of God and our standards that our Lord Jesus Christ was born of the Virgin Mary . . . that He offered Himself a sacrifice to satisfy Divine justice and to reconcile us to God . . . that on the third day He rose again from the dead with the same body with which He suffered . . . that our Lord showed His power and love by working mighty miracles." I am aware that Auburn Affirmationists have tried to stifle this noble testimony; but such efforts have been countered by the organization of an Orthodox and a Bible Presbyterian denomination as well as by a continuing testimony in the old organization.

In the Southern Presbyterian Church a similar testimony has been lifted. Our last General Assembly passed without dissent the following resolution:

"The General Assembly hereby declares that it regards the acceptance of the infallible truth and divine authority of the Scriptures, and of Christ as very and eternal God who became man by being born of a virgin, who offered up Himself a sacrifice to satisfy divine justice and to reconcile us to God, and who will return again to judge the world as being involved in the ordination vows to which we subscribe."

Calvinism stands for the crown rights, and, if you please, for the crown jewels of our King, for the vision of a God almighty in His grace, a God who bowed the heavens and came down for us men and for our salvation.

Calvinism teaches the sovereignty of God in the life and salvation of the soul, that is, the creature's absolute dependence upon God for religion, the sinner's absolute dependence upon Him for saving grace. Calvinism teaches not only the prevenience of the Father in creation and providence and of the Son in redemption, but as well the prevenience of the Holy Spirit in regeneration. Calvinism sees man dead in trespasses and sins and confesses that the sinfulness of that estate whereinto man fell consisteth in the corruption of the whole nature. Accordingly, we must look to God's grace—His common and His saving grace—for all the goodness and all the wisdom that blesses the lives of men.

However, there is a common attitude in our loved land magnifying the sufficiency of man. Perhaps the accomplishments of a new nation in clearing the forest, building great cities, exercising sweeping prestige, have turned our heads. All too often the American declares that he is the "master of his fate and the captain of his soul." This glorifying of man stressed natural ability until New England Calvinism ended in the semi-Pelagian theology of Taylor and Finney. It has shown itself in the Evangelical Arminianism which places the determination of salvation in the will of man by declaring that God votes for you, the Devil votes against you, and that you have the deciding vote. Their plan limits God's foreordination and His foreknowledge of the sinners who are to be saved, and, when logically developed, leads to a limitation of God's sovereignty also in the spheres of history and nature. Thus, Boston University — the acropolis of American Methodism— teaches a limited or finite God. On another side, the sovereignty of God in salvation is limited by dependence on ecclesiasticism, or sacramentalism, not only in the Roman Catholic, but as well in the Anglo-Catholic and the Campbellite movements. Calvinism locates the glory of regeneration neither in the will of the sinner nor of him who applies the water, but in the gracious will of God.

Even American Presbyterianism has witnessed several efforts to curtail the Calvinistic testimony to the sovereign grace of God and the particularism of His saving activities. A century ago the Cumberland Presbyterians mutilated the third and tenth chapters of the Westminster Confession, the one dealing with God's eternal decrees and the other with effectual calling. At the beginning of this century, the U.S.A. Presbyterians added new chapters on the love of God and missions and on the Holy Spirit as well as made other changes to secure union with the Cumberlanders. These two new chapters invert the Calvinistic *ordo salutis* by placing repentance before regeneration and declaring that every hearer has the privilege (private right) to accept the gospel. Our leading Southern Calvinistic scholar, Dr. S. M. Tenney, said of this inversion: "I did not know a babe could kick before the quickening, that a sinner could be induced to repent before regeneration. This *shows* the drift to Arminianism." R. L. Dabney wrote of the Arminians, "They make both repentance and faith precede regeneration; and therein is the dangerous feature. Let us say, with the Scriptures, that repentance and faith are both exercises of a regenerate soul" (*Discussions* I. p. 239).

In the Presbyterian Church in the United States, we have been in the midst of a serious consideration of revisions, many of which were apparently designed to turn the edge of consistent Calvinism. At least for the moment, those revisions which tended to obscure our distinctively Calvinistic testimony to the sovereignty of God and the depravity of man have been lost. A year ago it was widely publicized to the world that we had given up our doctrine of predestination. But the last Assembly rejected every change proposed in the third

chapter of the Confession and the parallel sections of
the catechisms except a purely verbal change of a *mere*
to an *alone* and thus maintained intact the Westminster
doctrine of predestination and preterition. It similarly
rejected the proposed changes in the doctrine of total
depravity and maintained the elect infant clause. The
battle may not be entirely over, but we thank God and
take courage. We pray that He may keep the church of
Thornwell, Dabney, Palmer, Strickler, and Webb true
to the grand particularities of the Reformed Faith.

Again, Americanism opposes Calvinism in placing
the emphasis in the church and in the kingdom of God
upon human activity. Human activism, social panaceas,
reform movements, have usurped the place of emphasis
Calvinism gives to God's grace, regeneration by the
Holy Spirit, and the threefold work of Christ. Even
the great Christian word "faith" is given a humanistic
content as a projection of our ideas on the cosmic
screen. One man defines faith as the soul's invincible
surmise, another as the triumph of imagination over
sensation, or as only imagination grown up; others as
the will to believe, as betting one's life that there is a
God, or as an experiment that ends in an experience.
All these definitions agree in this: they leave God, who
according to Calvinism is both the author and the object
of faith, out of the definition. One is thereby reminded
of current definitions of the kingdom of God, which
likewise omit God from the definition, defining the kingdom as an ideal social order or as a society of individuals motivated by love.

The Reformed Faith can meet this departure from
the truth of the Word by placing in the forefront of
our message that which Warfield described as one of
the three distinctive contributions of John Calvin to the

history of Christian thought, namely, the threefold work
of Christ as prophet, priest, and king. If we throw
Christ's present heavenly work in the forefront, magnifying His application of the redemption which He has
purchased for us with His own blood, we effectually
nullify the charge of a dead orthodoxy. As we magnify
Him, He will own His gospel with a quickening power
that cannot be denied. In place of the "liberal" emphasis on human activity, the recognition of Christ's
manifold workings puts the stress upon divine activity
in the church. Again, instead of losing our drive in
developing abstract principles many of our people do
not follow, we shall place the living Person of Him
who died for our sins at the head of our crusade for
truth and righteousness. And in place of human leaders,
or even of Professor Karl Heim's presentation of Christ
as the only Führer worthy of the confidence of His
followers, we shall present our Redeemer in the offices
that the Word ascribes to Him—prophet, priest, and
king. In seeing not only the crucified Christ, but as
well the ascended King; not only the historic, but as
well the present Lord, we are standing not only for
Luther's theology of the cross but also for Calvin's
theology of resurrection glory—a point of view toward
which current studies in eschatology seem to be moving.

In the depths of our need, there is an Advocate with
the Father, Jesus Christ the righteous, and He is the
propitiation for our sins. We can enter into the holy
of holies by the new and living way of His sacrifice
for us. Though our sins be as scarlet, they can all be
purged away in His precious blood, and our feeble
petitions will be heard, our unworthy tribute of praise
will be accepted in the Beloved. The High Priest of our
profession ministers in the true tabernacle which God

pitched, offering His own intercession on the basis of His one and sufficient sacrifice to cover our imperfect selves and worship, to sue out for us gifts of the Spirit, to grant us grace and mercy for every time of need. Verily, the voices of our prayers, praise, thanksgivings, confessions, and aspirations ascend and the angels of His grace, mercy, forgiveness, comfort, and hope descend through the heavenly Son of man. The reasonable ground for expecting the earthly worship of the triune God to continue rests neither in us nor in our organizations, however powerful they may be, but in the Lord Jesus Christ, Who in the power of an endless life abideth the heavenly High Priest. This Great Minister of the true religion ever liveth to intercede for His own. He is exalted a Prince and a Savior to give repentance and remission of sins, to write God's laws on our minds and hearts, and to remember our iniquities against us no more. And thus the blood of Christ cleanseth our conscience from dead works to serve the living God.

And this interceding Savior is the Lord at the right hand of God. The power of the Almighty is His power. All authority in heaven and on earth is committed to Him. When the forces of men lift themselves into a declaration of totalitarian might, then the church of Jesus Christ repeats her Confession of Faith in God the Father Almighty and in Jesus Christ, His only Son, our Lord, Who ascended into heaven and sitteth at the right hand of God, the Father Almighty. The Apostles' Creed, which steadied the martyrs as they faced an imperial Caesar, is again steadying the hands of our confessional brethren as they face totalitarian demands in Germany. The statement of these brethren written for Palm Sunday reads, "Wherever the gospel is preached in its purity, there is Christ our Lord. Our eyes are fixed on Him, not on the words and actions of men." With Christ there is a power greater than the powers of men; and trusting in the might of our King, we lift our testimony to Him. He Who was with our covenanting fathers will not forsake the banners lifted in His name; but by His victorious might will subdue unto Himself us and all His other enemies. The lusts of the flesh, the lusts of the eye, and the pride of life seduce; the forces of the Prince of this world rage around; but above the wrath of men and the rage of demons, "Thy throne, O God, is forever."

"The scepter of righteousness is the scepter of Thy kingdom." At the cross, Christ triumphed over the forces of hate and bitterness to ascend the throne of His glory. The powers of darkness did their worst, but "up from the grave He arose, with a mighty triumph over His foes." Today, clothed in all the panoply of God, He is guiding history toward the hour when He shall be manifested in the glory of the Father with the holy angels swelling the triumph of His return. Our King shall reign till He hath put all enemies under His feet. And that faith and hope lifts up the hands that hang down and strengthens the weak knees. "Sing, O daughter of Zion; shout, O Israel . . . Jehovah, thy God, the King of Israel, is in the midst of thee, a mighty One who will save" (Zeph. 3: 14-17).

Christ executes the office of a prophet in revealing to us by His Word and Spirit the will of God for our salvation. It has pleased the Lord, during a long and varied historical development, to reveal Himself and declare His will unto the church and to commit this, His own revelation, wholly to writing. Thus the Bible is the written Word of God with which the Spirit may forever abide, the instrument by which the Lord dispenses to believers the illumination of His Spirit. The former methods of God's revelation having ended, His present method of revealing Himself to sinners for their salvation is by His Word confirmed by the internal testimony of the Holy Spirit. Through His Word and His Spirit, the heavenly Prophet, our Lord Jesus Christ, speaks faith to our hearts. As Dr. Hugh Martin has well stated the matter: "Belief in Christ on the authority of Scripture is belief in Him on His own authority; being in fact the living flash of identification between the Word as written and the living voice of Him whose Word it is. I repeat that living faith is the living flash of identification of the written Word with the voice of God" (*The Westminster Doctrine of the Inspiration of the Scripture*).

Principal John Macleod gives this story from the life of his late colleague, Professor John R. Mackay of the Free Church College: "I saw nothing in myself but darkness, guilt, and pride. Then I remembered that Christ is a prophet who can dispel my darkness, a priest who can remove my guilt, a king who can humble my pride. And I said, surely, it were good that we two should meet." My friends of the Calvinistic Congress, it were good that we also should meet with this Prophet, Priest, and King; yea, and good that the America we love should likewise meet with Him Who alone can dispel her darkness, remove her guilt, and humble her pride.

GOD'S SOVEREIGN CHOICE OF THE YOUNGER SON

The Rev. Principal John Macleod, D.D.

The tale is told in England of a working painter who made part of his living by painting the signs for inns; that he was engaged to paint the sign of a hostelry that went by the name of "The Angel." His special achievement as a painter was not in the line of angels but of beasts of prey (and indeed "The Red Lion" was the champion figure of his art), in painting which he thought he excelled. When he was asked to undertake the painting of "The Angel," he hemmed and he hawed, but at last he accepted the commission. As he did so, however, he gave due warning to his clients that they must not be taken back if when the work was done "The Angel" should be like a "Red Lion."

So when an old hand at preaching takes in hand to deal with such a subject as we are to look at this evening, his hearers need feel no surprise if his lecture or address should turn out to be not unlike a sermon. Indeed, to be quite open and above board on the matter, the address I am to give you is pretty much an expansion of the notes of an old discourse that dealt with the sovereignty of God as it comes before us in the ninth chapter of the Epistle to the Romans and in par-

169

ticular as it is illustrated in the crucial instance of the twin sons of Rebekah, who were yet unborn. "For the children being not yet born, neither having done any good or evil, that the purpose of God according to election might stand, not of works, but of Him that calleth," it was said unto their mother, "The elder shall serve the younger" (Rom. 9:12).

THE ELDER SHALL SERVE THE YOUNGER

The teaching of the Apostle in this solemn and weighty chapter is that of the free sovereignty that God shows in the disposal of His saving blessings. All kinds of endeavors have been made to get him to teach something else than he does, or to shut out the definiteness of what he has to say in regard to the bearing of God's choice on the individual salvation of His people. When he speaks of the twin sons of Isaac and Rebekah before they were yet born and when they had as yet done neither good nor ill, the attempt is made to restrict the reference of his words to the two brothers as the representatives of the peoples descended from them. An election may be granted by such interpreters to special office or to national privileges. But they do what they can to shut out a reference to the personal, individual destinies of the twin sons of Isaac. Man has his old quarrel with the rights of God as a free Sovereign. He is not disposed to make the acknowledgment that grace is grace or that mercy or lovingkindness so belongeth unto God as that He may do as He will with His own. Man thinks that he has some claim upon mercy or that he gets less than justice when mercy is not shown to him. If he only took time to think of what the rights of God, his Maker, are and of what the evil of sin is, he might and he ought to see that, owing to its intrinsic and native turpitude, sin earns death, and the being who is guilty of sin has no right to look for anything as his own but what he has earned by his sin. Our Maker is not only our King and our Lawgiver; He is also our Judge; and because in His judicial character He gives to everyone as he has earned at His hand, the sinner cannot rightfully claim as his own anything else than that he should reap the fruit of the seed that he has sown. If, then, he gets what he has earned, it is only of God's mercy or of His undeserved goodness that this is so. The mercy that is shown him, whatever its measure, maybe is a thing that belongs only to God and He dispenses it freely as One who is under no obligation to those who get the good of it. So it is free bounty, and it is as a King who does as He sees right with what belongs to Him that God bestows it. In His mercy, then, which thus belongs to Him as His own, He is not only free but sovereign. It does not belong to any one sinner to grudge the good that his fellow gets nor should he dream that either his neighbor or he has a right to anything else than what is due of sin, for we as sinners are not entitled to have mercy shown to us, but the very opposite. It is then a legal spirit or a self-righteous vein that is found in the man, whoever he be, that thinks that he gets bad justice if he does not get as good as his neighbors. And it is at the bidding of such a spirit that men pick a quarrel with the doctrine of the Apostle when he teaches our absolute dependence on the sovereignty of the free grace of God.

What is indeed wrong with men and their thinking on this subject is that they give place to the thoughts that meet with the welcome from the race of mankind as they have fallen away from God and His thoughts.

The thinking of the flesh is enmity against God. It is
not subject to His law and indeed it cannot be. Until
the power of this mind is broken, men will think little
of sin even as they have low thoughts of God against
Whom sin is done. They think that His law is too high
in the standard that it sets, in the demand that it makes,
and that it is too stern and strict in the sanction with
which it avenges the breach of its precept. So they fail
to take in or to lay to heart what it is that they deserve.
Thus they do not see that they stand in need of a mercy
that they cannot merit; and they do not recognize what
the true nature of mercy is. They do not see that it
is a thing on which they have no claim however utter
and urgent their need of it is. In this way, they do not
feel that mercy is a thing that belongs wholly to God
and is at His absolute disposal. It would be no mercy
at all if He lay under any obligation to show it to the
unworthy. Grace would be no more grace if He were
bound to exercise it. Whether He is to show mercy lies
with Himself alone. And when He withholds it and lets
the doom of the law take its course, He is altogether
righteous. He is just out and out. And it is no blot or
stain on His glory that He should visit the ways of the
wicked upon their own heads. If only the heart of
man were loyal to his Maker and his King he would
own readily and without a grudge that the mercy a
sinner needs belongs wholly to God to extend it or to
withhold it as He sees right. He is under no bond of
obligation that would bind Him to relax the penalty of
His law and free the rebel from the forfeiture under
which he has come as the wages of sin. The disloyalty
and estrangement of the heart of the rebel is the fruitful
source of objections to God's holy judgments, and it
is only when the soul is set right with Him that it will

adore His majesty as He gives effect to the counsel of His own will.

We have in this portion of this great doctrinal Epistle a treatment of God's holy and adorable sovereignty that is fitted to try the temper of our heart by the response that we make to its truth. Mercy, as we have seen, in its very nature can be shown only to those who are unworthy of it. As far as desert goes, they deserve only that it should be denied them or that they should get what they have earned as their own. When God is pleased to show mercy on some, the undivided glory of it is His, and others have no ground for finding fault, for they get only what they have earned. On this last principle of giving men after their own work, the Father, Who is the Righteous Judge, will give to the last Adam after His work. So our Lord, as the Servant of God, will have the reward of His services of love, and thus those whom He died to redeem are to have the life that He died to win for them. The thing that is free to them is dear to Him. He finds the reward of His services in the blessing that is bestowed upon His ransomed ones. By His work, the claims of God, the Judge, are answered and honored so that in virtue of His Son's obedience unto death in the room and stead of His chosen people, He is just, and He is seen to be so when He justifies the ungodly who believe on the name of Jesus, our Lord, Who is the Lord, our righteousness.

There is in regard to His people a gloriously free working of the sovereign will of God. It is of Him that they are at all a people, for apart from His choice of them they would not be His people. They would in that case be left with those who are not His people, who live in sin and who die in sin as they have lived

in it. Among the seed of Abraham who were all, in
one sense, His chosen ones, there were those who were
but the children of the flesh as well as those who were
the heirs of the promise. Among the posterity of Jacob
himself, there were Israel after the flesh as well as
Israel after the Spirit. Those who had no more than a
flesh and blood standing in the house of God were not
the children of God. They were in the house and belonged to it, but the house did not belong to them.
They were highly exalted as far as outward advantages
go, but they were not the true people of God. In respect of means and opportunities and privileges, they
were greatly favored; yet when, in the fulness of time,
the true King of Israel came to His own whom He had
the right to claim as His own, His own received Him
not. They would not bow to His yoke nor would they
have Him to reign over them. There were found, however, among them a people prepared, a remnant whose
heart was turned to the Lord, their God, and they would
have Him. Such a mind was theirs because they were
born of God. These were the living seed of the covenant
people. They were not only of Israel: they were
Israel. Their fellows who would not have Him were of
Israel, but they were not Israel. This was so, for they
were not all Israel that were of Israel. Some who had
the name and the outward standing had no more: they
wanted the life that is distinctive of Israelites indeed.

In regard to one's being Israel indeed, the principle
held in the days of our Lord that has held through the
ages. It was to be seen in the house of Abraham himself. It finds utterance in the words, "In Isaac shall
thy seed be called." Those who were like Ishmael, the
son of the bond-woman, were not the children of God,
but the children of the promise were counted for a

seed. As there was an election in the household of Abraham that made choice of Isaac and set Ishmael aside, so there was another election in that of Isaac. Here there were two sons who were not only of the same mother but were twins, and this relationship was closer than that of Isaac and Ishmael. The one of these twins was chosen: the other was set aside. And the word of the Lord spoke to their mother as she was still bearing them, which told her that the elder should serve the younger. The purpose of God, according to His kingly counsel and choice, was to take effect. This choice was not made of works or good desert on the part of the one who was chosen. It was made known before they were born or had done good or evil. He who was chosen was not one whit better than his brother who was set aside. The thing in its last analysis resolves itself into God's choice. It is He as Sovereign who made the one to differ from the other; They were both alike sons of godly parents. That of itself would not save them. If it would save the one, it would save the other; but it would save neither, for they were both alike the seed of Adam after the flesh and as such were of the corrupt mass of fallen mankind. Thus they were sinners, and it was for the heavenly Potter to say whether either or both was to be left to reap the fruit of his sin and to be fashioned as a vessel or as vessels unto dishonor. If they were to follow the way of their fallen race, they would both be left to their sin and its doom. So it was for God to say if either was to be made a vessel unto honor. Before their birth He let His mind be known that He chose one of them for Himself and which of them that was. This meant more than that there was to be a vast difference as to outward privilege among their posterity.

It meant also that among the sons and seed of Jacob it was those of them that were chosen as he was chosen who were to be the people of God indeed. The principle of God's election is at work among nations and in their ranks among men as to the advantages that they shall have. But it comes closer home to personal salvation. It is according to God's choice, that each of His people is saved. "For it is not of him that willeth nor of him that runneth, but of God that showeth mercy." Here let us look at: I. What was common to the two; II. The distinction between them; and, III. What the elder was to do to the younger.

I. *What was common to the two?* If we begin at the beginning, we must say that they had a common nature, for the brothers both belonged to the one race of mankind. But to say this is not to bring us very far forward. They were, however, as we have seen, brothers; that is to say, they had the same father and mother. They had a common home, for they belonged to one of the families into which the race is divided. The parents these twin brothers had, both feared the Lord and had His blessing. They knew His name as He was pleased to make it known. Now, if grace ran in the blood, the sons of such a father and mother would have their share of it. Then it would be well with the two of them. But we must bear in mind that grace does not run in the blood, for the children of the flesh are not the children of God. It is not one's first birth of parents who are ever so godly that makes one a believer. There is a new birth needed, the fruit of which is the faith that brings a man into the number of the children of God. They are all the children of God through faith. Those only who believe are the adopted children of God, and it is as the children of the new birth that they believe.

It is that a man is born of God that accounts for his believing in His Son and so receiving Him and receiving in Him the right to be a son of God. The new birth is not the adoption, but the one makes way for the other. That the twins were the sons of the child of promise did not make them the children of God, but it gave them a godly home with all the advantages and good things that such a home brings with it. Yet the fact remained that they were not only the children of Isaac; they were also of the stock of Adam.

As Jacob and Esau were by their birth the seed of the first man, so are we all. We have seen that as the seed of Adam, they had the nature that is common to the race to which they belonged. This they had in common with all of us, and all of us have it in common with them. The bond that binds us to the first man bound them, too. Because of this, they and we are sharers in a common ruin, for it holds of the race as fallen. And it holds both of the doom that is out against the guilt of sin and of the hold that death has of the heart and soul of man as a child of wrath. The first sin of our first father is in its guilt the source of that spiritual death in which his children from their birth are involved. It is counted as theirs, and they reap the fruit of it, and this fruit is to be seen in the birth sin that is common to all who stood in Adam while he stood and who fell in Adam when he fell. What the Psalmist confessed they might each confess — that they were shapen in sin and brought forth in iniquity. So they started life with the taint of birth sin, and apart from what the grace of God does in the case of some, this is what holds good of high and low, of rich and poor, of white and black, of all the fallen race—that with such a start they will go on in sin.

If the two brothers shared in the general ruin of the race in regard to their standing and their nature, both, they were sharers in the same black outlook. That is to say, if they were left to themselves, they would share in a common destiny, for this they would carve out and earn as their own. If they were only the seed of Adam, fallen, they would of themselves choose the way of the world and those who take this, which is the course of the age, make their way to the death in which it finds its end. It is only the call of God that brings from death to life. This is needed that we may choose life and the way that leads to it. When He, in His saving grace, calls, He writes His law on the heart. Thus he bends the will to obedience and sets free the former rebel from the lordship of the mind, which is enmity against God. Men may have the same advantages of upbringing, yet in the end there may be a world of difference between them. It is when one's privileges are crowned with the blessing of saving grace that one gets the good of them. Nothing less than such a crown of blessing will make a sinner who is lost in sin a child of God. We see in regard to the two brothers that though they had much in common, they ran very different courses. There came in something that made a difference.

II. *The distinction between them.* It was a distinction, and it was more. It was a difference. There is a distinction between any two. Each is himself and neither is the other. In the case before us, there was a real difference. What made Jacob a new man made him differ from what he once was. This, too, made him differ from his brother. No doubt in the distinction between them there was a difference of natural bent. The one brother was of an active and stirring disposition; the other was quieter and steadier. Yet such a difference of natural disposition that marked their personal identity did not go so deep as to put one on the side of God and the other on the side of the world. This natural difference might serve through life to mark them out from one another in the eyes of their fellows, yet for all that they might both be children of the world. The real difference that emerges between them was because of the work of the grace of God, which called the one to newness of life while the other was left to his own ways. This call made Jacob a new creature. It made him differ not only from his brother but from himself as he once was. As the outcome of its work, he was not now what he once had been. So still God's gracious call parts His called ones from their own past as truly as it parts them from the fellowship of the world out of which it calls them. Esau went on in sin. So, too, would Jacob have done but for God's call.

The call that made Jacob a new man was the outcome of God's choice. That choice was not on the ground of prior goodness. It was plain enough in his case that, however quiet and orderly he might be, he stood in need of being made over again as a new creature if he was to be made a man of God. He showed by the kind of things that he did what a crooked twig he was: one that needed to have the twist taken out of it. He was chosen not for good that was in him. It was a choice that was all of grace, and it was one of the thoughts of God that were hidden in His secret counsel until He let it be known. The word of the oracle that spoke of him before his birth made it known as a thing that would yet come to light. It came to light when the set time came, when the providence of God had so wrought that His word was made good: and the elder served the younger. Until the set time came, the brothers were both alike—men of this world, the one more diligent and the other more daring. They were alike in respect to their privileges. Each had the best outward privileges that he could have in his day on earth. They would have to answer for it. They were alike by nature as sons of Adam, for they lay under the doom that is common to a sinful race and were held in the frost grip of a common estrangement from the life and love and fear of God. They were alike in the exercise of their natural freedom, sinners at their own hand. They took the way that pleased themselves; and if things were to go on as they had begun, they were both heading for one and the same end. The one end for which they were making was that for which sinners still make, for sinners are still what these brothers were in their day, the sons of fallen Adam, and as they take the way of sin, it leads them on to death.

When God's time of grace came, Jacob was called, and he lived. It was the call that made him what he had not before been, a new man. Until it came, he was but a natural man. He embroiled himself with his brother. This was his folly, and it was worse than folly: it was sin. The day of his distress came upon him. It was the fruit of his own short-sighted folly. He had to flee for his life. He was a homeless wanderer, an exile and an outcast, when in his misery God drew near to him. The call that he got was due to nothing in himself. If his brother was profane, it could not be said of Jacob that he was worthy or attractive or markedly amiable or straight. Yet on such a one, all unworthy as he was, God set His heart. It was only grace, free, unmerited favor, that was to be seen in this.

To the outcast as he slept at night in the open field, a vision was given in which he might see the mystery of mediation; words of precious promise and assurance were spoken to him. From that night onward when God spoke to him, the life of Jacob was other than it had been before. It was that of one to whose heart the Lord had spoken. He was alive from the dead, not yet what he was to be, but no more what he used to be. A change of nature was given and with it a change of standing. The new man Jacob was forgiven and blessed in spite of all the hard things that fell to his lot. He had not himself to thank for all the blessing that was now his, for he was no better than his brother. Each was a sinner and, on the ground of merit, each had earned the same doom. If either were to be dealt with after his merit, the law would have taken its course and each would have been left to reap as he had sown.

III. *What the elder should do to the younger:* He was to serve his younger brother. The younger was to be uppermost. He was to be lord, and his brother should serve him. Now, if the elder only took this well and was willing to serve and was glad to do so, he would be the true master. It is the way of the world, that men aim at mastery over their fellows so that others shall serve them. We seek to lord it over others. Such is not the way of the kingdom of God; and when Jacob learned to say to himself, "Thy servant Jacob," he made headway in the direction of being master indeed. The true Master, when He came, came not to be ministered unto but to minister and to give His life a ransom for many. He was with men as One that served. It is the way of men that the younger should serve the elder. In the case of the twin son of the heir of promise, this was to be reversed. And in the fulness of time the

Elder Brother served his younger brother. It was of God that Jacob was to be the master. The priestly privileges and sacred rights that belonged to his fathers were to descend in the line of his posterity.

What took place in the family of Isaac holds good still in the soul history of those that are his true seed. Each was no better than an Esau by nature and each comes to be a Jacob, nay, an Israel by grace. They, as was Jacob, are called, and God's quickening call brings them to a true life. As new men, they have a new life to live. They are then no longer what they once were. The soul of each is a field of battle, for in the Shulamite there is to be seen, as it were, the company of two armies. The new life has to grapple with the old nature. If now, the law of God is in the mind, the law of sin is still in the members, and these two laws are at war in the soul. As the war goes on, there are many ups and downs. Though at times the law of sin may trip up the man of God and throw him on his back, yet the grace that has been given is not to be overcome. It has come to reign and not to be reigned over. On the whole, it gives tone and direction to life. Yet here on earth it does not sweep the field. There is still left, though it may be only in lurking-places, the law of sin, the mind of the flesh, which is enmity against God, as it is not subject to His law but ever rises up against it. Yet the ruling bent of the man of God, though the old nature still lingers on, shows which of the two laws has the upper hand. "The elder shall serve the younger." It shall be kept subject to it, however much this may go against its grain. This is so because when grace comes it comes to reign. It is not to be trodden under foot. Pricks may be in the eyes and thorns in the side, but the land shall be that of Israel. The child of God is indeed a new creature.

What holds of the believer as one man holds of the fellowship of believers. They are a mixed crowd. At times the hangers-on may assert themselves so as for a season to be the masters of the situation. The mutineers run the ship. The end, however, is not yet. The ship shall be taken from them and those of them that are not hanged at the yard-arm are put in irons or hide in holes. This may not please them. They may grumble that the profession of the truth of the gospel is bondage for them. They feel as if they were put and kept in a straight-jacket when they feign submission. The calling, however, of the church to be a witness for God will yet be vindicated. In the end of the day, victory is sure for the seed of Israel. This holds in the case of the individual and in that of the community both.

As of old, so will it be again. The bondwoman and her son are to be cast out. As for Gad, it was said that a troop should overcome him, but he should overcome at last. So is it with each of the seed of the kingdom. Though they should be overborne, they shall overcome in the end. So, too, will it be of the kingdom itself, for all who offend will be cast out and the just will inherit the land. Thus the purpose of God in His choice will stand. He has purposed, and He will make it good. His promise and His Word will be fulfilled. And when the elder will serve the younger, it will be seen that the counsel of God's heart, which is the word of His mouth, will stand fast as do His thoughts from age to age. His way is in the sea and His path in the great waters. His footsteps are not known, for His judgments are unsearchable and His ways past finding out.

AND HUMAN RESPONSIBILITY

The Rev. Dr. L. Greenway

When Dr. Hoogstra and his committee, last November, invited me to address this conference on the subject of "God's Sovereignty and Man's Responsibility," my first inclination was to decline the invitation. I felt then, and still feel, my inability to make a substantial contribution to a discussion that has engaged profound minds for centuries. Upon further consideration, however, I became persuaded that it might be helpful if I should take this opportunity to reaffirm some of the more practical truths involved in this subject without dealing directly with the apparent antinomy it presents. In an age when men are trying to conform their theology and ethics to the measurements of their hatbands, it is not likely that we old-fashioned Christians can insist too strongly upon the fact that man was created to live responsibly in a universe over which a sovereign God presides. There will always be occasion for a Calvinistic conference so long as the wisdom of this world rearranges the wording of my subject and makes it read: "The Sovereignty of Man and Divine Responsibility."

It is not necessary to spend much time defining the terms in my subject. I believe the best definition of the sovereignty of God was uttered by a heathen. I am

184

referring to the words of Nebuchadnezzar recorded in Dan. 4: 34-35:

"And at the end of the days I Nebuchadnezzar lifted up mine eyes unto heaven, and mine understanding returned unto me, and I blessed the most High, and I praised and honored him that liveth forever, whose dominion is an everlasting dominion, and his kingdom is from generation to generation: And all the inhabitants of the earth are reputed as nothing and he doeth according to his will in the army of heaven, and among the inhabitants of the earth: and none can stay his hand, or say unto him, What doest thou?"

As for the term "human responsibility," I should say that it is intended to express this truth: *Man by creation is a moral creature capable of moral judgment. As such he is fully accountable to his Creator for all his thoughts, words, and actions. The foundation of his accountability lies in his original endowments.*

It is immensely important that we have the right mental attitude toward this subject. My observation is that the people who become indignant toward the truth of God's sovereignty most generally are people who are proud and irreverent. There is no want of material in this discussion to inflame their wrath. Just because the "modern mood" is characterized by its unwillingness to receive anything of an authority ulterior, exterior, and superior to the individual, it is the more urgent that we emphasize the need of humility in the treatment of this subject. It has been said of the typically modern man that the less another has to do with him the more comfortable he feels. That is the spirit of self-sufficiency and independence. When that spirit is dominant within us, we are unfit for a profitable discussion of this tremendous issue. Here, then, is caution we must impose upon ourselves at the very outset. Let us recognize the limitations of our understanding, and, what is more,

let us keep God sovereign in the discussion, for after
all, it is His sovereignty that establishes the fact of
man's responsibility. If God were not sovereign, man
would be independent. And if man were independent,
then, paradoxical as it may sound, he would not be
man, for it is the glory of human nature that it was
made to serve the glory of its Maker.

One more remark by way of introduction. The people
who object to our cast-iron conception of God's sovereignty and man's responsibility do not reckon sufficiently
with the historical fact that Calvinism has produced,
with an amazing regularity, strong men, strong women,
and strong nations. As Carlyle says: "Calvinism has
produced, in all countries in which it really dominated,
a definite type of character and conception of morals
which was the noblest that had yet appeared in the
world." We are charged with embracing a tyrannical
faith. Shallow minds describe our system as "dreadful,"
"paralyzing," "fatalistic," "antinomian." But how
strange that such a system should produce the ethical
heroism of which the Reformed Faith is characterized!
The consistent Calvinist has always represented a strenu-
ous morality. He has never forgotten that his election
is unto holiness. Exceedingly jealous of the honor of
his Lord, he displays a measure of moral energy and
aspiration that confounds his critics.

I

Calvinism is the only system of doctrine taught in
the Bible. We accept that system because we accept
the Bible as the authoritative Word of God. When,
therefore, we are asked to establish the facts of God's
sovereignty and man's responsibility, when we are challenged to show that the one does not rule out the other,

we promptly turn to the Bible, and we are not embarrassed for want of evidence. Both facts are repeatedly set forth in Scripture. Let us consider two of the references.

In the opening chapters of Exodus, we have the familiar narrative of the conflict between Jehovah and Pharaoh. In Exod. 4:21, we read:

"And the Lord said unto Moses, When thou goest to return into Egypt, see that thou do all those wonders before Pharaoh, which I have put in thine hand: but I will harden his heart, that he shall not let the people go."

No less than ten times is it stated in these chapters that the Lord hardened Pharaoh's heart. But it is also stated repeatedly that Pharaoh hardened his own heart. In Rom. 9:17, God says to Pharaoh:

"Even for this same purpose have I raised thee up, that I might show my power in thee, and that my name might be declared throughout all the earth."

Here are the two facts as clearly stated as any fact can be—Divine sovereignty, human responsibility; God's immutable decree, man's unforced choice. God sovereignly hardened the monarch's heart, yet that monarch remained accountable and deserving of punishment. Pharaoh was not compelled to act against his own choice. What he did he did voluntarily. In fact, he boasted of his freedom; he shouted defiance of God's authority: "Who is Jehovah, that I should obey His voice to let Israel go?" (Exod. 5:2). Some people insist that Pharaoh never had a chance. He was the victim of circumstances over which he had no control. He was helpless in the face of the fixed divine decree. The Lord hardened his heart. But wait a moment. The fact that the Scripture clearly presents both sides of the issue requires us to keep a balanced viewpoint of the matter. A few weeks ago, I spent a forenoon raking leaves in preparation for a little gardening in the back-yard of my home. When I had completed the task, I noticed that I had developed some calloused spots on my hands. How did that happen? Obviously, by the friction of the rake handle. I was the victim of a certain universal law that has to do with physical impact and friction. Who established that law? God did. Then it was God who produced these calloused spots? Unquestionably. But who did the raking? I did. Then it was I who produced these spots? Unquestionably. I accepted the responsibility of hardening my hands when I exposed them to the operation of a universal law established by God Himself. So Pharaoh voluntarily, responsibly, hardened his heart when in the face of repeated warnings he defied a universal moral law.

The greatest crime ever committed was the crucifixion of the Son of God. Closely associated with the perpetration of this crime was the foul deed committed by Judas Iscariot. It is not necessary to review the story of his treachery, but I do want to direct your attention to his remarkable confession recorded in Matt. 27: 3-5:

"Then Judas, which had betrayed him, when he saw that he was condemned, repented himself, and brought again the thirty pieces of silver to the chief priests and the elders, saying, I have sinned in that I have betrayed innocent blood. And they said, What is that to us? see thou to that. And he cast down the pieces of silver in the Temple, and departed, and went and hanged himself."

Note again that confession: "I have sinned . . . I have betrayed innocent blood." It cannot be questioned that Judas spoke rationally and truthfully. He took the right view of his conduct; he had adequate grounds for his self-condemnation and despair. He had sinned. He had not been made to sin. If he had been made to sin, he would have been conscious of it and would most certainly have seized upon the fact as a basis for excusing himself. What he had done in betraying innocent blood he had done freely and voluntarily. He does not say that he had been unfortunate, that he had been the victim of fate or the irresponsible tool of a higher power. Nothing of that is in his confession. Instead, he says, "I have sinned, I have betrayed innocent blood." Judas Iscariot admits his guilt without pleading any excuse. He recognizes his responsibility for a crime that has brought down upon his head everlasting infamy.

Now, keeping that in mind, let us turn to Peter's sermon on the Day of Pentecost. Speaking of the crucifixion of Christ, Peter says:

"Him, being delivered by the determinate counsel and foreknowledge of God, ye have taken, and by wicked hands have crucified and slain" (Acts 2:23).

This statement, mark you, covers also the part which Judas assumed in the criminal transaction. "The determinate counsel and foreknowledge of God," which made certain our Lord's death on the cross, includes all the steps that led up to the event as well as the event itself. By "wicked hands," our Lord was betrayed and slain. Here, then, two separate, distinguishable agencies coincide to accomplish one purpose: divine decree, human choice; God's sovereignty, man's responsibility— forming like two separate cords the unity of a knot. Formal logic says the knot cannot be tied. But look! The knot is tied. Philosophy says, "I cannot understand this; it's beyond my scrutiny." That is exactly the truth. Philosophy does not have a ladder high enough to reach the altitude where these two facts combine in perfect harmony.

> *Bid, then, the tender light of faith to shine*
> *By which alone the mortal heart is led*
> *Unto the thinking of the thought divine.*

II

It is instructive to observe that in the regular routine of our workaday life we do not ordinarily allow the mysterious coincidence of divine sovereignty and human responsibility to disturb us much. We are solemnly certain that God's secret will shall be accomplished but at the same time we find it most practicable to keep our hands on the wheel. Since leaving Michigan Monday afternoon, I have driven by many farms and have seen scores of farmers working in their fields. I am sure that at least some of these farmers heartily accept the doctrine of God's sovereignty, but that conviction does not keep them out of their fields. If it is God's will that they shall have a crop, it is no less God's will that they shall be instrumental in producing the crop. I might have stopped along the way and invited them to attend this conference. I might have said to them, "Gentlemen, we are having a conference in Paterson, New Jersey, and the theme of our conference is 'The Sovereignty of God.' Why don't you come along? God is sovereign. Whatsoever He purposeth shall come to pass. So you may as well leave your fields to His discretion." I can imagine one of those robust farmers replying, "Stranger, we have State institutions for people like you." So, with respect to the practical issue of our daily labors and activities, we just naturally assume our responsibilities. However certain we may be as to the immutability of the divine decree, no one

of us is disposed to make a caricature of that truth by
saying, "The Almighty made the universe, and He
is responsible for it. I shall not attempt to interfere
with His prearranged plans. I shall simply remain
passive and allow God to manipulate me as He sees fit."
It is only when we transfer this discussion to the realm
of grace that we meet with bitter criticism and scorn.
Here we are charged with embracing a doctrine that
teaches, at least by implication, that if a man is destined to go to heaven he shall go there regardless of
his wicked conduct, and that if one is destined to go to
hell, he shall go there regardless of all his strivings to
enter heaven. The opposition waxes most bitter at that
point where Calvinism insists that the sinner's inability
to do good and to be good does not relieve him of his
responsibility. Though he has destroyed his ability, he
has not destroyed his obligation. The responsibility continues along with the inability. Note how the Heidel-
berg Catechism presents the matter:

"Q. 9. Doth not God then do injustice to man, by requiring
from him in His law, that which he cannot perform?

"A. Not at all: For God made man capable of performing
it; but man, by the instigation of the devil, and his own wilful
disobedience, deprived himself and all his posterity of those
divine gifts."

To those who say that if depraved man is unable to
keep the law he is not obliged to keep it, we reply with
the following Scriptural and reasonable propositions:

1. By way of illustrating our doctrine: In the business world, a merchant's inability to settle a debt he has
contracted does not release him from the obligation in-
curred by that debt. He cannot truthfully say to his
creditor, "I owed you yesterday because I was able to
pay you, but today I owe you nothing because I am
unable to pay you anything."

2. In all our thought upon this subject, we must ever keep in mind that the sinner's inability to obey the divine law was not imposed upon him by the creative power of his Maker. God made man upright, and in this state of rectitude, man had "freedom and power to will and to do that which is well-pleasing to God." The sinner's present bondage and helplessness constituted no part of his original righteousness but it came upon him through his own free act of apostasy and rebellion. He cannot, therefore, release himself from his responsibility by charging his present impotence upon God.

3. Though this impotence is the result of the sin of Adam, contemporary man is responsible because God imputes the sin of Adam to all his posterity, in virtue of the fact that humanity is an organism.

4. The result of sin cannot excuse the sin itself. In this connection, allow me to read an illuminating statement from Rousseau's *Confessions* (Book II):

"The sophism that ruined me was precisely that into which the generality of persons fall who lament the lack of resolution, when it is already too late to exercise it. It is our own fault that uprightness is difficult; and, were we but always prudent, we should rarely have occasion for the virtue of prudence. But propensities that are easily surmounted lead us unresistingly on; we yield to temptations so trivial that we despise their danger. And so we insensibly fall into perilous situations, from which we might easily have preserved ourselves, but from which we now find it impossible to extricate ourselves without efforts so superhuman as to terrify us, and we finally fall into the abyss, saying to the Almighty, 'Why hast Thou made me so weak?' But, notwithstanding our vain pretext, He addresses our conscience, saying, '*I have made thee too weak to rise from the pit, because I made thee strong enough not to fall therein.*'"

Bound up with this whole discussion of inability and responsibility is the subtle Arminian doctrine of man's moral freedom. The doctrine, briefly stated, is this: If, in any action, man had power to will what he did, or not to will it, in that action he is free (cf. Reid, *Essays*, IV, 1). With this as his major premise, the Arminian argues that the Calvinistic doctrine of God's effectual, irresistible grace subverts the morality of man's actions and makes him a machine acted upon by another being. In reply to this, the Calvinist says that *man's moral freedom is the ability to follow the tendencies of his own nature. Man is free so long as he does what he wants to do. Under no circumstances can man expect more freedom than that.*

III

The question is often asked, "What is the use of preaching the gospel if men are 'dead in trespasses and sins' and are unable of themselves to respond to the call of the Word?" That question is not hard to answer. From Scripture, we learn that it is part of God's plan to use the elect to call out other elect. Preaching is as much a part of God's decree as is sovereign election. This is the mainspring of Christian missions. It is a guarantee of missionary success. To know that God has ordained the service of preaching to be a means of bringing men to repentance gives great zest and encouragement to the minister of the Word. He knows that when he preaches that Word he is handling imperishable goods. Moreover, he is assured that the Word is the grand instrument of the Holy Spirit, Who gives efficacy to the gospel call. The Calvinist believes in preaching to dry bones, not because he has any confidence in these bones but because he has all confidence in the living, eternal God.

It was not revealed to the writers of the New Testament nor is it now revealed to the ministers of the gospel, who are the elect. "The Lord knoweth them that are his"; but He has not given this knowledge to any of His servants. Nevertheless, in obedience to His command, they "go into all the world, and preach the gospel to every creature." And whenever difficulties or dangers oppress them and they are tempted to despair of their venture, they recall the sublime prophecy of their Lord:

"Other sheep I have, which are not of this fold: them also I must bring, and they shall hear my voice; and there shall be one fold and one shepherd" (John 10:16).

Notice, the Lord does not speak of them as "other creatures" or "other goats," but as "other sheep." They are already His sheep, His people, though they have not yet been brought in. But they shall be brought in. They shall hear His voice. And in that day, when many shall have come from the east and the west to sit down with Abraham and Isaac and Jacob in the kingdom of heaven, there shall be one flock and one Shepherd.

Wondrous sovereignty of God! Blessed responsibility of man! Let us never attempt to pry into the *secret* will of our sovereign God. That can never serve as the starting-point for our thinking or the norm for our acting. In all the relations of life—civic, political, moral, religious—our starting-point and norm is the *revealed* will of God. From that *revealed* will we learn that it is our responsibility to preach the gospel to every creature, to apply the mind of Christ to every legitimate sphere of action and influence in which men move, and to walk as those whose pilgrimage is on earth but whose citizenship is in heaven.

"The secret things belong unto the Lord our God: but those things which are revealed belong unto us and to our children forever, that we may do all the words of this law" (Deut. 29:29).

AND THE WORD OF GOD

The Rev. Prof. G. Ch. Aalders, Th.D.

THE SOVEREIGN GOD is a ruler over not only unreasonable and purely material creatures, but He created also reasonable and moral creatures, over whom He exerts His sovereignty. This He does, according to the reasonable and moral character He has granted unto those creatures, by revealing unto them His will. He speaks unto them His Word; He gives them His commands; He acts as a legislator. This implicates the responsibility of these creatures and so the subject of this address fits in with the forceful and fine address we heard yesterday-night.

Now, the Word of God, which He as their Sovereign speaks unto man as a reasonable and moral creature gifted with responsibility, comes to us in written form in the Holy Scripture, in the Bible. And it will not take much of our understanding to realize that this written Word of God, the Bible, as the law of the Sovereign of heaven and earth, is sovereign also. This Word of God is absolutely authoritative, and it cannot be otherwise. Therefore, the authority of Holy Scripture always has been a matter of the greatest importance unto Calvinism, one of the most outstanding features of

Calvinism, to confess this authority most fully and firmly and to stand for it with all its energy.

In our days it is necessary to point out that Calvinism, therefore, cannot be satisfied with the attitude taken by the renowned German, or rather Swiss theologian, Karl Barth. Surely he acknowledges the sovereignty of God and likewise the sovereignty of the Word of God; he even does not hesitate to call Holy Scripture the sovereign Word of God, and in his writings many beautiful passages are to be found concerning this point. But the same Karl Barth declares that the Bible is subject to human criticism and this to the very end. He expresses himself in this way: that we not only have to listen humbly and obediently to the Word of God, which is Holy Writ; but that we have to listen on the other hand quite as well to human criticism of Holy Writ, yea, that we have to allow the human criticising word concerning Holy Writ to pronounce itself to its full extent. To me, and I think to you all, these two things seem utterly incompatible—if Holy Scripture is the sovereign Word of God there is no room left for human criticism; if we allow human reason to criticise Holy Scripture, it cannot be authoritative. Barth seeks to combine these two wholly incompatible statements by the way of the *paradox*. Now I am not going to enter into a discussion on the Barthian paradox-theory; the only thing which seems necessary with respect to the point I am referring to, is: to investigate whether Scripture itself induces us to take the Barthian attitude. Scripture itself teaches us God's Sovereignty and man's responsibility—two things which are incompatible, as far as our human reason can see — but we accept these two unhesitatingly because we clearly observe that Scripture teaches both. Now we have to put the question: How

about the authority of Scripture? What is the statement made by Scripture itself? Does it claim on the
one hand absolute authority, and allow on the other
hand our full criticism? I think it can easily be proved
that Scripture demands our absolute submission and
does not leave any room whatever for our criticism.

To prove this, we refer to Jesus Christ. If any one
would ask us to give in a very few words a circum-
scription of the contents of Holy Scripture, our answer
ought to be: Jesus Christ. He is the messages of Scripture to a sinful world. Now to give in brief lines an
idea of the authority Scripture is claiming for itself we
surely may ask: How did Christ regard Scripture? Then
we see, that Christ repeatedly refers to Scripture with
the announcement, "It is written." This is, according
to the way in which He expresses Himself, the end of
all contradiction. One of the most remarkable instances
is the temptation of the Savior by the devil. Three times
He refers to Holy Scripture in answer to His tempter:
"It is written." This decides the matter absolutely, and
we observe, that even the devil after that had no answer.
So even the devil has to acknowledge the decisive character of the appeal to Scripture: Scripture has absolute authority, and there is no room for any criticism,
even by the devil.

In the same way the Savior often says, "Have you
not read" or "Scripture says." The New Testament
is full of such quotations. and in John 10:35 Christ
declares that "the Scripture cannot be broken." In
claiming authority unto Holy Scripture He does not restrict this to the main ideas, or to the words, but He
deliberately declares that "one jot or one tittle shall
in no wise pass from the law," i.e., from Holy Scripture (Matt. 5:18). The *jot* is the smallest consonant of

the Hebrew alphabet, and with the *tittle* we have to understand the different small hooks and angles by which the Hebrew consonants are discerned from one another. Here we see that Christ extends the authority of Scripture to the very letter.

With this testimony, His practice is in full harmony. In John 10: 34-36 and Matt. 22: 31, 33 we find two illustrative examples showing how the Savior argues upon a single word (the word *elohim*—gods, and the names of the patriarchs). And in Matt. 22: 42-45, His argument over against the Pharisees is based on the simple fact that in Ps. 110 the Hebrew has *adoni*, with the one letter which indicates the possessive pronoun of the first person, "*my* Lord."

These examples deliver the strongest proof that our Lord Jesus Christ meant the authority of Holy Scripture really to be an authority even to the letter; which most certainly excludes every idea of human criticism.

In this way we have to follow Christ. And if any one might object that this only regards the Old Testament, we answer that this surely must be admitted, but both Testaments are one and what holds for the Old certainly holds for the New. Furthermore, the authority of the Old Testament has been to a much larger extent subject to criticism than the New; so if the Old Testament is safeguarded by the judgment and the example of Christ, how much more the New Testament.

Now, with respect to the authority of Scripture, we have to realize that such authority can only be ascribed to that which is exactly the *meaning* of Holy Scripture. It is necessary to point to this, because there often has been a wrong use of Scripture, e.g., the practice of some people who, in order to receive an answer by Scripture to some question, in a haphazard manner opened the Bible and took the first verse their eye rested upon as the answer of God, which forced them to many a queer interpretation of such a verse. This cannot be the right way. Surely, Scripture has absolute authority, but this authority is that of the *meaning* of the words used.

I wish to show the significance of this statement with regard to two points.

The first has to do with the difference between literal and figurative language, a difference very well known to everyone of us. In using the expression, "My goose is cooked," we are quite well aware that there is no goose whatever present and that it has nothing to do with any cooking at all. So Holy Scripture also may contain figurative language, and of course we have to understand such language according to its *meaning*. I referred to Scripture as the law of the Lord, but this law is not wholly given in a form of a legislation. Surely, Holy Scripture contains legislative parts, especially in the Old Testament (remember the Ten Commandments); but the greater part of the divine sovereign law is given in the form of history and poetry and prophecy; and naturally we have to regard the *meaning* as authoritative. Everybody will realize that it is necessary to undertake a careful and prayerful investigation in what sense every Scriptural expression is *meant*. No one is permitted to take a figurative expression literal nor to explain a literal statement as though it were figurative.

The second point is one that has to do with a difficulty many Christian people have had to face in discussions with unbelieving and worldly men. Such unbelieving people like to point to Joshua 10: "Sun stand still"; and then they argue: We know that not the sun but the earth is moving; so this is a mistake, which shows that

Scripture cannot have divine authority. But the Lord has given His Word not only to scientific men, but also to very plain and simple people. Therefore, Scripture speaks the plain and simple language of every-day life and knows not the scientific terminology of scholarly men. Even the astronomer in daily life says, "The sun is rising," though he is quite aware of the fact that the sun is not moving and only the earth is revolving upon its axis. In this simple terminology of everyday life, the miracle that happened in the days of Joshua is described, wherefore it is said that the sun stood still.

In connection with the authority of the Bible, there is yet another fact. The authority of Scripture does not depend upon the human authors, but upon God, Who is the prime author of Holy Writ. Decisive is not which human author wrote this or that section of the Bible but decisive is: God inspired the human author, whosoever he may have been, by His Holy Spirit to write what He wanted to make us know. Therefore, in investigating the human authorship of the different sections of the Bible, we must keep this in mind. We have to stand for the absolute truth of everything which is related in Holy Scripture; but it is not necessary to accept, for instance, the Mosaic authorship of the Pentateuch in this sense that he wrote the five books assigned to him from the very first to the very last word. We have to acknowledge that he gave the law to Israel because that is explicitly said in Scripture, but we are not bound to believe that he wrote the account of his own death in chapter thirty-four of Deuteronomy—for Scripture does not say that he did.

Calvinism stands for the absolute divine authority of the Holy Scripture; and Calvinistic scholars have to defend this authority over against human criticism, especially with regard to the Old Testament. There is a large opportunity for these scholars today. For there is a most remarkable turn of the tide in Old Testament criticism, as I pointed out in my inaugural address as a professor of Old Testament exegesis in the Free University of Amsterdam, in 1920. And this turn of the tide has been going on ever since. A large number of assertions made in former days by Old Testament critics have now been disapproved by scholars of absolutely critical attitude. Old Testament scholarship has found itself in the necessity of acknowledging the truth of many a Biblical statement, which it most deliberately denied before. This presents a large opportunity to Calvinist scholars. But they are in need of your co-operation by your prayers and by the buying and reading of their books. And may the Lord give His blessing, that also this labor according to the never antiquating, "Soli Deo Gloria," be to the honor and glory of His Name.

CONFERENCE TRANSACTIONS
KINGDOM EXTENSION IDEALS

RESOLUTION

"The Calvinistic Conference expresses its sincere appreciation for the kind invitation extended to it by the Board of the Christian Sanatorium, Goffle Hill, Midland Park, N. J., and for the friendly entertainment provided for it at their luncheon.

"The Calvinistic Conference wishes to assure the Board of its deep interest in this particular field of Christian benevolence, and pledges to the Board its sympathy and its moral support for this institution" (Resolution adopted at Conference Dinner in the Christian Sanatorium).

LETTERS

June 12, 1939

To the First American Calvinistic Conference

FELLOW CALVINISTS:

I deeply regret that a speaking assignment at the International Conference of Evangelical Student Unions at Cambridge University, England, precludes my attendance upon the sessions of your Conference.

I am writing these lines on the way to England and wish to assure you that though I expect to be present both in body and in spirit at the Cambridge Conference from June 27 to July 3, I shall at least in spirit also be present at that time in Paterson. May your meetings be a source of strength and inspiration for all who in our country love the Reformed Faith. May the banner of the God-centered interpretation of the Christian Faith which we associate especially with the names of

205

Augustine, Calvin, and Kuyper be lifted up anew and many with us find in it strength and comfort and beauty!

Forward in faith!

Fraternally yours,
CLARENCE BOUMA

June 27, 1939

THE REV. DR. JACOB T. HOOGSTRA
American Calvinistic Conference
Paterson, N. J.

DEAR SIR:

In the name of the Free Magyar Reformed Church in America, a strict Calvinistic Church body, I send my warm greetings and good wishes to the sponsors and partakers of the First American Calvinistic Conference.

I deeply regret that owing to the fact of our rapidly approaching synodical and church constitutional meetings to be commenced on July 2, we cannot attend in a larger body but at the same time I am glad to know that Dr. Charles Vincze of Perth Amboy will be present.

It is high time that in the present turmoil and conflict of ready-made isms, when blood and race, political systems and states, even human beings, are deified, the everlasting sovereignty of God — this preëminently Christian thesis — should be emphasized with the firmness and clearsightedness of Reformed Christians.

I hope that this first Calvinistic Conference will be crowned with success and will render the war cry for all those earnest believers who—as in the days of Elijah—have not bowed unto Baal.

Sincerely yours,
ALEXANDER DAROCZY
Arch-Dean, Free Magyar Reformed Church

FRIDAY MEETING

Held in the Paterson Y. M. C. A. June 30, 1939

Among the many things that were acted upon the last day of the Conference, the following remain of lasting importance:

The Rev. J. J. Hiemenga reports as delegate to the Mid-Western Ministers' Conference which met in Grand Rapids, June 8, 9, 1939. He reports that the Mid-Western Conference has a committee to arrange for a national conference in Grand Rapids in 1941.

Resolution presented by Dr. C. Vincze in organizing a permanent Calvinistic Association. Motion prevailed to place this resolution in the hands of a committee to report to the Eastern Ministers' Conference. Also a general resolution in favor of this idea was adopted by the Calvinistic Conference. This resolution was also referred to the same committee.

Dr. Charles Vincze now introduces the subject, *The Future of Calvinism*.

THE FUTURE OF CALVINISM IN AMERICA

The Rev. Dr. Charles Vincze, Ph.D.

1. CALVINISM is the "solid food" in Christendom. It cuts through the surface in every respect and follows the lead of God's revelation to the roots and the essence of everything. In respect to humanity, it is like the outspoken physician who tells the patient in unwrapt words just what is wrong with him. Calvinism does not believe in make-believes. No towers of Babel, no achievements of the natural man can allure it into catering to his pride. Calvinism is the eternal "No" to all human conceit and self-complacency. It tells the little sinful man who is bursting with pride that compared with his original and "in Christ" embodied estate he is *totally depraved*, incapable of essential and lasting good, unless created anew by the One Who is alone good, the originator and upholder of the universe. Thus Calvinism throws man down and thus Calvinism makes God the measure of human aspiration. No wonder that the humanists of all times always find Calvinism a stumbling-block and that Calvinism can never make peace with the humanists. And as the humanist way of reasoning is always more apt to flourish in the so-called prosperous times, Calvinism will always en-

counter difficulties in such periods. Its real opportunity always comes in times of crises, it is always more welcome after rock-loosing earthquakes, illusion-shattering windstorms, conceit-burning fires. Other forms of Christianity might satisfy the so-called "religiosity" of the natural man but when one is confronted with the real "to be or not to be" dilemmas of existence, then the straight shooting of Calvinism is as welcome as a wound-scratching, honest, benevolent, clean hand. As crises, bringing home to us the impasses of all purely human efforts, form an organic part of the universe as we know it, Calvinism has a cosmic basis for an opportunity to carry its message to humanity, an opportunity to lay a siege to all sorts of Babels and to build altars to the true God. I believe in the future of Calvinism, first, by virtue of one of its supposedly objectionable points, *total depravity*.

2. Then, Calvinism is here to save humanity from the plight of the poor woman who was diseased for a long time and had suffered many things of many physicians and was nothing bettered but rather grew worse. Calvinism saves us from falling victims to spiritual quackery. It points us directly to the God-granted Physician and medicine, the Lord Jesus Christ. It does not take us to supposedly miracle-working shrines but right to the miracle-working Miracle Himself. It does not attempt to lengthen the always already twelve years' duration of our sickness by taking us around in a gallery of saints and semi-mediators, but it hastens us to the only Mediator Himself. It does not obstruct the way of the cure-seeking penitents by leading them through the chambers of quasi-courtiers of a Medieval monarch all represented as expecting some spiritual gratuities, but it opens the way right to the presence

of the King and it warns everyone not to share the honor and trust due in its fulness to the King alone with anyone. Calvinism is consequential. It tells us that apart from the Lord Jesus Christ there is no salvation, and it wants us to live up to it. "The death of the Son of God is the only and most perfect sacrifice and satisfaction for sin, and is of infinite worth and value, abundantly sufficient to expiate the sins of the whole world." Calvinism offers nothing of its own invention. Calvinism simply offers what God Almighty "has been pleased of His infinite mercy to give, His only begotten Son, who was made sin, and became a curse for us and in our stead, that He might make satisfaction to divine justice on our behalf." I love Calvinism because it does not aspire to anything but to bring me into a *direct, personal, immediate communion* with my God-given Savior, in Whom if I believe, God granting me faith, I "shall not perish, but have eternal life." *This type of Christianity can never perish from the face of the earth.* The Fathers of Dordrecht were right when they stated that "this promise, together with the command to repent and believe, *ought to be declared and published to all nations, and to all persons promiscuously and without distinction." As* I believe in the reality of our "sickness unto death," *as* I believe that real sickness ultimately rejects anything but the real remedy, *as* I believe that the Lord Jesus Christ as crucified is the only remedy, and *as* I believe in the effectiveness of the proclamation of His gospel, so I believe in the future of Calvinism.

3. Finally, I observe that the "remnant" of the Old Testament prophecies made a decisive and lasting impression upon Calvinism. It studied, meditated on, and searched after the mysteries surrounding it, more than

any other type of Christianity. How is it that God
has never been left without any witnesses, that a remnant always remained faithful even in the midst of
national and wholesale corruptions? How is it that
some are attested in the Bible as children of salvation
despite all the revelries of sin around them and how
is it that some are branded as the children of perdition
despite the seemingly most favorable conditions and
the doctrine of free, sovereign election emerged from
these penetrating meditations and careful searchings of
the Word of God? *Our salvation is not a matter of our
choosing.* Although "the death of the Son of God is
the only and most perfect sacrifice and satisfaction for
sin, and is of infinite worth and value, abundantly
sufficient to expiate the sins of the whole world," it
does not include everybody in such a way that it would
depend upon our decision to take it or leave it. To
dispense with the saving graces of His own Son, God
reserved in His own counsel, absolute free will and
grace. "I will have mercy on whom I will have mercy.
and I will have compassion on whom I will have compassion. So then it is not of him that willeth, nor of
him that runneth, but of God that showeth mercy."
*Christ's atoning sacrifice does not constitute a break
in God's sovereignty.* It is really the most convincing
demonstration of it. No work of the Son can lessen the
dignity and authority of the Father. No sinner can cir-
cumvent the godhead of God by misappropriating the
Son. Christ came to bring us to the Father and not to
exempt us from under the Father's authority. Even
His atoning sacrifice, although "abundantly sufficient
to expiate the sins of the whole world," was meant and
offered for the redemption of those whom the Father
pleased to elect. "For this was the sovereign counsel

and most gracious will and purpose of God the Father that the quickening and saving efficacy of the most precious death of His Son should extend to *all the elect,* for bestowing *upon them alone the gift of justifying* faith, thereby to bring them *infallibly* to salvation; that is, it was the will of God that Christ by the blood of the cross, whereby He confirmed the new covenant, should *effectually* redeem out of every people, tribe, nation, and language, *all those, and those only,* who were from eternity chosen to salvation and given to Him by the Father," that He should confer upon them faith, which, together with all the other saving gifts of the Holy Spirit, He purchased for them by His death; should purge them from all sin, both original and actual, whether committed before or after believing; and having faithfully *preserved them even to the end,* should at last bring them, free from every spot and blemish, to the enjoyment of the glory of His own presence forever. This purpose, proceeding from everlasting love *toward* the elect, has been from the beginning of the world to this day powerfully accomplished, and will henceforward still continue to be accomplished, notwithstanding all the *ineffectual* opposition of the gates of hell; so that the elect in due time may be gathered together into one, and that there never may be wanting a church composed of believers, the foundation of which is laid in the blood of Christ; which may steadfastly love and faithfully serve Him as its Savior and which may celebrate His praises here and through all eternity.

Well, here is Calvinism in its most characteristic doctrinal features. Here are *unconditional election, limited atonement, irresistible or efficacious grace, and the perseverance of the saints.* They are quoted right from their most authoritative statement, from the Canons of Dort, the essence of which is embodied in those liturgical questions of public confession, which every Hungarian Reformed Christian must answer in the affirmative and in a loud voice before he can be admitted to the Lord's table. There can be no more awe-striking nor inspiring sight under heaven than a Hungarian Reformed congregation answering those questions in unison: "This I do believe and profess." We feel ourselves at the threshold of the Holy of Holies when we make that public confession, which is really the reaffirmation of our first confession of faith and of our confirmation vows. And what gives us such a spiritual uplift when we answer those terse questions whole-heartedly? *The realization that our God is God.* God all the way through. There is no break in His sovereignty. He is the same uninfluenceable sovereign Lord in the orbit of the cross as He is over all the recesses of material creation. His lordship is unquestionable; His sovereignty acknowledged; His wisdom confessed. For it was wisdom on His part not to let the efficacy of His beloved Son's blood-purchased salvation depend upon our whim but to condition it upon His decree and to back it up with the fulness of His divine power and thereby make it the "sure salvation" of His elect. In this way our faith does not rest on any human "wisdom" but on the power of God. And it is infinitely better to depend upon His mercy and power than upon any of our imagined good works, merit, or righteousness. It is the only way in which a foretaste of heaven is given. I believe in the future of Calvinism in America or anywhere else because it teaches of a God Who is really God.

RESOLUTIONS, DISCUSSIONS

The Rev. Prof. G. Ch. Aalders, Th.D., of the Free University of Amsterdam, was the speaker at the Conference dinner. In his speech, he compared Dutch Calvinism with American Calvinism. He indicated briefly some of the achievements in the Netherlands, among which was the founding of a free university, free within creedal limits. He took account of our different historical, social, and ecclesiastical antecedents and consequent emphases. At the same time, Dr. Aalders felt that the immensity of the task should not be the standard of our endeavors. Simply because times and seasons are against us, obstacles should not deter us from marching onward. Our standard is the command of God. Although we, therefore, will have a rough road ahead of us, obedience to the sovereign God is the only and the sufficient warrant to forge ahead.

Although Dr. C. Vincze had suggested this earlier in the day, the resolution of the Rev. J. J. Hiemenga was enthusiastically adopted. "Resolved that we, the members of this first American Calvinistic Conference, held in Paterson, N. J., on June 27-30, 1939, dedicate ourselves to the ideal of a Calvinistic University in America, and that we pledge our wholehearted coöperation to the realization of this ideal."

Resolutions as adopted by conference for further study, "Be it and hereby it is resolved, that the First American Calvinistic Conference appoint a Committee for the organizing of a Federation of American Calvinists.

"The purpose of this Federation will be:

"1) To rally the scattered forces of American Calvinism first on an individual basis;

"2) To arrange regional and national Calvinistic conferences, and promote fellowship among the adherents of Calvinism."

NOTE: The Conference Program Committee has instructed its secretaries, the Rev. Jacob Van Bruggen, and the Rev. Jacob T. Hoogstra, to edit these *Proceedings*. The Rev. Jacob Van Bruggen left suddenly to occupy a mission post at Crown Point, New Mexico. Urgency demanded haste. The entire responsibility, therefore, fell upon the other member of the committee.

JACOB T. HOOGSTRA

SPONSORS

Beets, The Rev. Dr. H.
Berkhout, Dr. Peter B.
Bogert, Mr. J. V.
Borst, The Rev. L. J.
Bosch, Dr. T.
Bouma, The Rev. Dr. Cl.
Bouma, The Rev. Hessel
Broekstra, The Rev. M. E.
Christie, Mr. P. M.
De Haan, Mr. Peter
De Leeuw, Mr. Peter
De Vries, Mr. Albert
Denkema, Mr. Henry
Egedy, Mr. Gerrit
Englewood Chr. Ref. Church,
  Sewing Circle
  Ladies' Aid
Hamilton, Mr. Cornelius
Hekman, Mr. Henry
Hiemenga, The Rev. J. J.
Hoogstra, The Rev. Dr. J. T.
Jaarsma, Mr. R. C.
Keyser, Mr. Frank
Keyser, Mr. Peter
Kuipers, Mr. Wm. R.

La Fleur, Mr. Sipp
Peters, Mr. A.
Petzinger, Mr. Lambert
Sisco Dairy Co.
Sisco, Mr. S.
Soodsma, Mrs. Christina
Stap, Mr. Barney J.
Supply, Mr. H.
Tanis, Mr. Jacob
Tanis, Mr. James
Tanis, Mr. Leonard
Touw, Mr. Lambertus
Van Bruggen, The Rev. Jacob
Vande Kieft, The Rev. J. M.
Vander Snow, Mr. Barney
Van Genderen, Mr. C. P.
Van Hoff, Mr. Diederik
Van Vlaanderen, Mr. John C.
Veenstra, Mr. Abram
Verblaauw, Mr. Peter
Vermeulen, Mr. Abram M.
Vermeulen, Mr. David
Westervelt, The Rev. J. A.
Willey, The Rev. Dr. J. H.
Wyngaarden, The Rev. Fred

Printed in United States of America